THE SCIENCE OF MUSIC

The Science of Music

ROBIN MACONIE

CLARENDON PRESS · OXFORD

1997

Oxford University Press, Great Clarendon Street, Oxford OX2 6DP

Oxford New York
Athens Auckland Bangkok Bogota Bombay
Buenos Aires Calcutta Cape Town Dar es Salaam
Delhi Florence Hong Kong Istanbul Karachi
Kuala Lumpur Madras Madrid Melbourne
Mexico City Nairobi Paris Singapore
Taipei Tokyo Toronto
and associated companies in
Berlin Ibadan

Oxford is a trade mark of Oxford University Press

Published in the United States
by Oxford University Press Inc., New York

British Library Cataloguing in Publication Data
Data available

Library of Congress Cataloging in Publication Data
Maconie, Robin.
The science of music / Robin Maconie.
p. cm.
Includes bibliographical references and index.
1. Music—Philosophy and aesthetics. 2. Music—Acoustics and
physics. 3. Music and science.
ML3800.M237 1997 781—dc20 93–43398
ISBN 0–19–816648–6

1 3 5 7 9 10 8 6 4 2

Typeset by Hope Services (Abingdon) Ltd.
Printed in Great Britain
on acid-free paper by
Biddles Ltd.,
Guildford & King's Lynn

For
Alys

Preface

Getting started

In *Greek Science* Benjamin Harrington said:

There is no human knowledge which cannot lose its scientific character when men forget the conditions under which it originated, the questions which it answered, and the function it was created to serve. A great part of the mysticism and superstition of educated men consists of knowledge which has broken loose from its historical moorings. (Harrington 1961: 311)

Explaining music in words is a paradoxical task. Language has the function of widening the field. It allows a meaning in music to be expressed that would otherwise remain hidden, but to imagine that it confers meaning on music would be a mistake. Only by attempting to reconcile language and music are we likely to discover where language ends and music begins. The distinctions of music are a part of spoken language, and the limits of music notation have a great deal to tell us about the limitations of print as a medium.

The idea that language is necessary for thought has focused attention on the nature and structure of language in relation to our knowledge of the world. That in turn has led from time to time to strange conclusions, for example, that without language, thought is impossible; or, if the words don't make sense, the thought is meaningless; or, that perception follows grammatical rules; or again, if there are no words to describe an experience, the experience doesn't exist. 'Philosophy is not concerned with what *enables* us to speak as we do, but what it is for our utterances to have the meanings they have,' remarks Michael Dummett in *Origins of Analytical Philosophy*. 'It is essential to describe language as a conscious activity of rational creatures. If you were giving a description of human language to some Martians who knew nothing about human beings you would have to explain that to them, or they would not know what sort of phenomenon it was' (Dummett 1993: 187–8). You see my problem. If there is a meaning to music, it has to do with with the part played by acoustic distinctions, in human utterances and perceptions, in the maintenance and preservation of individual continuity. Other people are part of that continuity. Meaningful speech—including analytical philosophy—belongs to that part of human living that co-opts other people into the self-preservation process. The function of music, however, embraces all perceived and generated sound signals, including drumming fingers on the table, saying 'um' and 'er', rap, swearing, and laughter. Martians told that language is the conscious activity of rational creatures, observing human language in action, would conclude from that remark that it was an activity human beings themselves did not consciously understand.

Belief in a one-to-one correspondence between language and thought (and by extension, between language and reality) has further interesting implications. It can lead to a conclusion that new thinking is impossible, because new words by definition are inconceivable. New thinking can only be a rearrangement of pre-existing concepts, since the only new words that can be validly used are combination terms or new terms for old words. It is not possible to have new concepts because that would entail inventing words in advance of having the concepts, which is a nonsense. Furthermore, if word and thought are indivisible, the position is unclear about error. The legal profession makes a living out of advising on such delicate ambiguities as arise when words are true and the thought mistaken, or words false and the thought (as expressed by the consequential act) contradictorily blameless. Finally, the idea that language is instrumental for thought is unable to account for people learning to think in the first place, since the correct use of language requires thinking as a prerequisite, and by definition without language thinking is impossible. It means that such fundamental questions of human existence as How do I know who I am? How do I recognize the existence of an exterior world? and How do I learn to think? are either tautologous or nonsensical. It also follows that those unable to express themselves in language, for whatever reason: deafness, muteness, being a foreigner, being an animal,

physical disability, extreme youth, lack of education, or depriva-
tion—have until recently been considered as a matter of principle
to be intellectually as well as socially disadvantaged. Such views
have been around for a long time. They do not make the task of a
musician any easier.

The difficulty of making a case for the existence of a world independent of words and their meanings is especially acute for thinkers
whose primary mode of discourse is words and their meanings. It
is for this reason above all that musicians have the task of defending music as a serious intellectual pursuit. Composing and performing music is what we do best, but simply writing and playing
more music is not going to bring its explanation any nearer. The
goal is to explain why music should be taken seriously, in language
that readers can understand. Practising musicians are not trained to
do this, and professional scholars are not inclined to get involved in
areas outside their range of competence. The psychology of music,
for example, is both isolated from the mainstream of psychology
and out of touch with the ideas and meanings expressed by real
composers in actual works in the concert repertoire.

Explaining music in musical terminology is not enough.
Musicians acquire a language of signs and symbols for reading and
writing, and a body of conventions for interpreting them. These
codes of communication are perfectly adequate in a musical context, but of no practical use in explaining music to non-musicians
for whom the terms are unfamiliar and the underlying concepts
unproven. It is not that people don't want to know, or that musicians are unwilling to explain. Music's appeal is a great mystery, and
there is enormous popular interest in uncovering its secrets. But
poverty of language has always stood in the way of understanding,
which is why interviews with famous musicians so often disap-
point. (There are exceptions: Stravinsky, Stockhausen, Cage,
Debussy come to mind.) The reader begins to wonder why top
composers and conductors, people who demonstrably know what
music is about, seem unable to express themselves in intelligible
language.

Part of the difficulty musicians have in explaining themselves
must lie in the fact that after the Renaissance the practice of music

became increasingly disconnected from the practice of philosophy. Prior to 1600, music was at the leading edge of intellectual life. It evolved in close association with science and technology. New instruments of music were developed for experimental purposes and not only to suit the requirements of performers and composers. Today the glamour of music has to do with the celebrity status of a privileged few whose talents are the object of public fascination. It has no longer to do with the intellectual credibility of the musical profession, which is part of the reason why its leading figures so often appear out of touch and unable to defend themselves, most notably on the subject of contemporary music. Great performers display a peculiar attachment, under pressure, to antique terminologies of earlier, authoritarian times. They talk about music as the manifestation of spiritual currents and submission to powerful emotional forces which it is their ecclesiastical right to interpret and the poor listener's duty to accept without question. This is language intended to deter rather than to encourage debate. Of course, a misuse of philosophical or psychological language by musicians does not mean that the terms themselves are without meaning, only that their meaning has to be sought elsewhere. At least the possibility of meaning remains. Our objective is simply to reconcile the motives and perceptions of musicians with the real concerns of intellectual life, and with common sense. Since the human apparatus of hearing has remained the same over time, and human perceptual and communication needs are also relatively constant, explaining music in modern terms is likely to throw light in turn on earlier more recondite terms of reference.

Among the great achievements of Western music, by common consent, one would name masterpieces such as the Bach B minor Mass, Mozart's *Magic Flute*, the Beethoven Ninth Symphony and the Berg Violin Concerto. Asked to name the great achievements of Western civilization, people are more likely to give an entirely different set of answers: democracy, science, the industrial revolution, the theory of relativity, the computer. Society makes the distinction between artistic achievements, which impress us with their aesthetic truth, and achievements in science and technology that impact directly on real lives in a real world.

Our first task is to face up to the reality that the two worlds of art and science are not mutually exclusive but deeply interrelated, and therefore that the concerns of music and science throughout history have shared common objectives that can be articulated in a common language. Belief in a separation of music from other expressions of human knowledge and achievement has been deeply ingrained in Western culture for over 2,000 years. In *The Concept of Music* I introduced the idea that music should be considered and studied in a wider context of human activity and interests, from the starting-point 'what is music really about?' The present volume asks a related, but different question: 'if music were not about "music" as it is usually understood, what would it be about?' The answer is found in the language and thinking of other departments of Western intellectual and practical life. Western civilization springs from a culture of the ear. The phenomenal world was originally construed in acoustical terms. Laws of nature were discovered in the structured behaviour of vibrating systems, demonstrated with the aid of existing and newly developed musical instruments, and expressed in terms that created an intellectual framework for understanding the universe. Harmony, temperament, resolution, and organization are all musical terms. The science of Pythagoras is a science of musical acoustics. Plato's prescription for an ideal city state is based on a concept of musical aesthetics derived from Pythagorean science, and owes its persuasive force to a determined, even sceptical refusal to budge from musical principles. The ancient philosophers were concerned to discover correspondences between the reality of a world accessible to hearing and the evidence of a world accessible to sight.

A better understanding of the acoustical world-view is able to throw light on residual features of oral belief systems that a modern visual or literal culture is unable or unconcerned to comprehend. Musical knowledge can at least show how it may have been possible for rational minds, from ancient times to the present day, to defend views of an outwardly irrational or superstitious kind, from the music of the spheres to doctrines such as reincarnation and transubstantiation, and from the myths of scripture to folklore and nursery rhymes. The truth of particular doctrines is not the issue:

what matters is the fact that such mysteries coexist with science, and are debated among intellectuals as either complementary or mutually exclusive systems of belief. Current debate has long ignored the acoustic dimension or the musical subtext of a great many hitherto 'irrational' convictions.

From infancy our understanding of the world develops as a co-operative relationship of aural and visual perceptions, of which hearing is initially the superior sense, because it comes ready-made and fully functioning, whereas seeing has to be learned. The ostensible basis for co-operation of hearing and vision is the idea that the audible world is fully congruent with the visual. That was not always the case in the context of past systems of belief, and is not always the case even today in respect of much of ordinary life. The older we grow, the more intellectual life becomes focused on a visual understanding of the world and our relation to it, to the neglect and detriment of aural modes of reasoning as they survive in music, in religious doctrine and in folklore. The literature and traditions of present-day Western philosophy and psychology are grounded almost exclusively in visual concepts of reality and verification. An established undergraduate text in psychology, in its seventh published edition in 1993, devotes just three out of more than 1,100 pages to auditory perception, and none at all to the perception of music. This is not an extreme example, but a fair representation of current academic priorities.

There are hard lessons to be learned from an intellectual tradition that ignores the evidence of an acoustical world-view, as represented in ancient literature and embodied in music of every time and culture. Such a tradition is profoundly unscientific; it leaves modern thinkers ill-equipped to understand those aspects of rational belief that reflect aural, as distinct from visual realities; finally it fails to address fundamental differences between aural and visual-based science, arising from the physical differences of hearing and sight. Hearing is omnidirectional; vision is directional. Hearing is permanently in focus; vision is continuously changing in focus. The sound world is intermittent and subject to decay; the visual world appears continuous and permanent. The world of hearing is necessarily dynamic; that of sight is necessarily static and apparently instantaneous. The two senses give rise to versions of reality that are not bound to coincide, and are frequently contradictory. These are consequential matters. When Aristotle and his medieval disciples declare stasis to be superior to motion, it is in part a declaration of the superiority of the reality of vision to the reality of hearing.

The science of music is an applied understanding of the world inferred from acoustical phenomena, their perception and retention, and practical functions. The practices of music, and design of musical instruments, represent that knowledge in a pure and rigorous form. The ordination of pitch into modes and scales can be understood as a manifestation of a greater organizing principle. The notation of music can be interpreted not only as aesthetic communication but also as information management. The repertoire of composed music in written and recorded form remains to be studied as a vast archive of acoustical science. By understanding music's place in human development, we enlarge our view of science, as well as gaining a better understanding of the intelligence and value of individual musical genius.

R.M.

Wellingborough, 1994

Contents

ᘰᘯ

List of Figures

1

Intermittency

DOES music matter? The short answer is yes it does. Music matters because it would have happened anyway. What does it matter? Music is a blanket term for human activities in organized acoustics. These activities include passive listening as well as active creation and performance. Acoustics matters because human beings can hear, just as chemistry (oenology, medicine) matters because people can and do recognize smells and in consequence develop the knowledge to do something about them. The same motivation to organize sense experiences produces the discriminations that nurture art, literature, and, dare I say it, philosophy. The relatively distinguishing feature of music is that perceptions of the sound world organize themselves rather differently from visual, olfactory, or grammatical perceptions. So music is interesting because it reveals the distinctive priorities of audition and auditory reasoning, and especially interesting in a cultural context that finds it necessary or amusing to ask such a question.

For music to matter it has to exist. We can deal with that later. Music exists, for the purpose of the moment, in the character and organization of sounds, and is latent in manuscript, disc recordings, and human memory. To say that music matters is to assign a value to musical practice, and in this sense the question can be dealt with in terms not of music in particular but of human activity in a more general sense. Activity matters because if we didn't do something we would all be extremely bored, or vicious, or both.

Does the experience of music matter? The music industry seems to think so, and aesthetics is hardly the music industry's main concern. What is important to those who manufacture television sets, compact disc players, and interactive video machines is software.

Software is the equipment's reason for existing, and music is a significant ingredient of software production. Music doesn't add to the functional utility of news television or computer games. Not much, anyway. But it acts as a continuing reminder of the capacity of equipment to function, and performs other menial tasks as well, as a lubricant for the user-machine interface, or identification for a quiz show. If the question is, does that matter? the diffusion of second-rate music throughout the world of communications certainly suggests that it has a role to play, if not *qua* music, then certainly *qua* something else. My own view is that music is much more interesting *qua* something else, as the art of winemaking is more interesting than bingeing on premiers—or even fourth or fifth—crus. Music is interesting as a continuing reminder of the functioning capacities of our (human) hearing and related thinking equipment. The trade-off is that the instrumentation and style peculiar to music of different origins and periods identify particular auditory priorities, and these in turn are linked to intellectual priorities. The advantage of music over the written record as a source of information about other times and other cultures is that music is relatively freely expressed and generally resistant to manipulation by political or academic interests.

There is a further philosophical dimension. In his paper on Piero della Francesca and Renaissance art J. V. Field compares the innovations of perspective in art and tempered tuning in music. Mathematical techniques derived from the science of optics provided painters with the basis for an exact depiction of spatial relationships in depth, but for various reasons (such as the need to satisfy more than a single viewpoint in practice) painters were in the habit of distorting true perspective to achieve a dramatic or pleasing effect. Musicians on the other hand were interested in the scale divisions of acoustic space, and were faced with a stark choice between a scale of ideal consonances but limited possibilities of key change, and a scientific equal-temperament scale that was mathematically exact but acoustically and philosophically impure. The price of freedom of key movement was the loss of the harmonic principles on which music had been based, not to mention the sin of embracing scale divisions based on an irrational number (the square root of 2). Field draws an ironic distinction between 'the importation of exact mathematical techniques into painting (where they were practised inexactly) and the unavoidable use of approximate mathematics in the practices associated with the allegedly exact science of music theory', and goes on to observe that the relationship between mathematical theory and artistic practice has been unjustly neglected by historians of art and science:

Remedying this deficiency is of interest not only as aiding understanding of the intellectual map of an important historical period but also in the more specific matter of understanding the part played by mathematics in the development of natural philosophy. . . . For instance, there is a total absence of discussion of the philosophical problems that Aristotelian philosophers generally saw as besetting the use of mathematics (Field 1993: 93–5).

As a link between mathematical theory and acoustical and physiological realities, musical scholarship clearly has a contribution to make, both to the history of mathematics and to the philosophical issues that attend mathematical speculation. For that contribution to emerge musicology will have to take greater account of musical acoustics, mathematics, and philosophy than it does at present.

Music also matters in effect because I say so, as the ancient gods by saying so caused things to exist and events to happen, thereby accounting to superstitious mortals for why things are as they are. Among aural cultures, sound signifies existence. Babies cry, dogs bark, water trickles, whips crack. The sounds of nature are self-referential. We perceive them as different and learn in time to associate their different qualities with differences in their make-up. Wood sounds different from tin, the squeak of leather from the ping of a microwave timer. Some sounds are continuous, like the hum of air conditioning or the ripple of a stream, but they are exceptions. Most sounds are intermittent and ephemeral, and because of this the aural concept of reality is framed to account for the continuing existence of things that may not always be signalling their presence in the world by making a noise of some kind. It is a world of hearsay. What the gods know for certain, said Homer, men know only by rumour (*Iliad* 2. 484 ff., cited in Huffman 1993: 125).

As the gods decree, so too does music, in the sense that what is heard to sound, by the same token is known to exist, and exist not just for the moment, but in a continuous present. A dog barking signifies not that the dog comes into being at that particular moment, whether or not it exists for the listener for the first time at that moment. The gods by saying so cause something not just 'to be', but 'to have been existing', which, to preliterate minds less attuned to the passage of time, is the same as causing something to come into existence instantaneously. The creation myth is about affirming the way things continue to be, or have been, which should come as a relief to theologians grappling with the consequences of taking the story of genesis literally.

All the same, my saying that music matters does literally change the situation. It creates the possibility that I may be right. This is not the same as making me responsible for it being right, in the way that a benevolent divinity is commonly held 'responsible' for creating what is intelligently affirmed to exist. My being right is not the issue here, because if I am right then music matters absolutely. Indeed, asking the question creates the possibility of an affirmative answer, to give credit where credit is due. But of course the question relies on what a reader conventionally understands by 'music' and 'mattering', while implying that in the sense that we understand things that matter, music as we understand it may not matter. It becomes a question of understanding: are the beautiful and decorative things in life truly useful or could we do without them? And beyond that, do we really know what matters?

In defending music I may be supposed to be defending the decorative arts as morally good and ultimately of value, and by extension endorsing the views of those who make a career out of defending the comfortable life. I am doing nothing of the kind. Music is more than decoration, and there is no necessary moral value in the merely decorative. I stand by Herbert Read in the belief (expressed in Read: 1953) that decoration should follow form. But Read said 'good decoration', and that is a value judgement, so perhaps there is a moral dimension after all. Read understood that decoration pursued for its own ends led designers and their patrons to ignore the structural principles to which decoration was originally intended to draw attention.

No, the point of my defending music is not to defend the beauty of beautiful objects, and only partially to defend the sense of beauty in music as an expression of useful faculties of discrimination. The art of music is of value inasmuch as it affects our understanding of the world of sound and what that understanding allows us to do. In my experience this is not quite what philosophers have in mind. What they have in mind is finding a legitimate excuse for listening to Mozart, and they like to do so by professing an allegiance to Schopenhauer, which again is not quite the same thing. Defending a love of music, which is a great source of anxiety to many intellectuals, is not the same as defending music itself, to which the same people are often manifestly indifferent. It would be encouraging if real composers and real music were occasionally the issue, but that is seldom the case. Philosophers from Plato onwards have expressed a cultivated disdain for real music. Professing Schopenhauer is no excuse for ignoring Cage. It is no part of philosophy's role to legitimize a weakness for music.

It is in music's gift, however, to restore meaning to philosophy where meaning has been lost. Aristotle's *Posterior Analytics*, for example, gains in intelligibility if a reader bears in mind the tension that exists, for the Greeks, between the acoustically and the visually verifiable. That sense of philosophy mediating between competing realities has nowadays largely disappeared, and it is not surprising if Aristotle's meaning is sometimes hard to find, as in the following passage which reasons from the transitory nature of acoustic evidence:

If the propositions from which a deduction proceeds are universal, then it is necessary for the conclusion of such a demonstration, i.e. of a demonstration *simpliciter*, to be eternal. There is therefore no demonstration of perishable things, nor any understanding of them *simpliciter* but only incidentally, because nothing holds of them universally but only at some time and in some way. . . . Hence you cannot deduce [from such a case] that anything holds universally but only that it holds now. The same goes for definitions.

Demonstration and understanding of things that come about often— e.g. of an eclipse of the moon—plainly hold always in so far as eclipses are such-and-such, but are particular in so far as they do not occur always. [75b] (Aristotle 1994: 13)

Jonathan Barnes remarks of the first paragraph that it is 'scarcely intelligible', and concerning the eclipse, 'obscure' and 'uncertain'. As translator of the passages, his view of his own understanding of them is certainly privileged; however, there are clues of an acoustic relevance that may have been overlooked here. The phrase 'perishable things' for example may be taken as referring primarily to sounds, which do not remain, but die away. To adduce that eclipses 'do not, fortunately, *always* occur' (Barnes in Aristotle 1994: 134) is also to miss the point that certain events, in the nature of things, are intermittent, meaning that they do occur from time to time, but not continuously. Barnes contends that Aristotle 'wishes to construe universal propositions as requiring the eternal existence of their subjects'. I don't think so, because Aristotle's chosen examples do not point the reader in precisely this direction. Eclipses are demonstrably intermittent: their definition includes intermittency as a condition of their existence. However, it surely follows from the predictable nature of eclipses, and Aristotle's other recurrent example, thunder (an acoustic event, interestingly enough) that these events are incidental to greater universal and eternal propositions, which can only be guessed at. (It is also in the nature of such obscure universals that they postulate an ongoing, *dynamic* universe.)

To a listener, as distinct from a (silent) reader, Aristotle appears to be saying that if the grounds of an assertion are universally true, a simple assertion is demonstrably and necessarily always true. For example, stone is hard; this stone is hard. This does not hold of transient phenomena, as for instance, this apple is fresh; all apples are fresh. It is demonstrably true of an apple at a particular time, but not true of any apple indefinitely, nor of all apples at any one time. Though we take it to be true of all apples that each is fresh at a particular time, that is because freshness is incidental to being an apple. The same is especially the case with sounds. The demonstrable qualities of a sound, e.g. that it is loud, clear, of distinct pitch etc., are incidental expressions of the instrument being made in a certain way, and being competently played. That a particular trumpet sounds in this way does not mean that it or all trumpets will always sound in this way, or that it will continue to sound the same note in an identical manner. The instrument has a range of sounds, all of which are typical of the trumpet, and the individual sounds themselves do not last indefinitely.

Musical sounds can be recreated, however. They can be regarded therefore as expressing 'intermittent truth', which may be the same point as Aristotle is making with the example of an eclipse, which is an event reproduced as and when the conditions of its occurrence recur. For an assertion to be intermittently true it is sufficient that the conditions of its occurrence arise from propositions that are continuously and universally true: in the case of an eclipse, from the motion of the earth in relation to the moon and sun; in the case of a musical sound, from the principles of acoustics that ensure certain consistencies of performance in a musical instrument from one note to the next. Of course, this guarantee of consistency is subject to human performance factors that may vary from note to note: intonation, pitch, loudness, and so on. (Insistence on absolute continuity of experience as part of the formula for belief in a continuous existence can also be overdone. I am not aware, as it happens, of any serious doubt in respect of the world continuing to exist even though you and I have to blink from time to time.)

From grasping that something is continuous (e.g. a note of constant pitch) one may progress to an understanding of some things as eternal (e.g. frequency of vibration of a stretched string as a constant in relation to length, gauge, and tension):

To know what something is and to know the explanation of whether it is are the same, and the account of the fact that something is is the explanation. . . . We plainly cannot grasp what it is to be something without grasping that it exists; for we cannot know what something is when we do not know whether it exists. But as to whether it exists, sometimes we grasp this incidentally, and sometimes by grasping something of the object itself—e.g. of thunder, that it is a sort of noise in the clouds. . . . In so far as we grasp that it exists, to that extent we also have some grasp on what it is.

There is a difference between saying why it thunders and what thunder is. In the one case you will say: Because the fire is extinguished in the clouds. But: What is thunder?—A noise of fire being extinguished in the clouds. Hence the same account is given in different ways: in one way it is a continuous demonstration, in the other a definition. [93a–b] (Aristotle 1994: 56–8)

Aristotle makes a general point about human response and a general point about language. To ask 'what is thunder' is to ask to what experience a word refers, assuming that since the word exists, it must correspond to something in reality, as words do not arise for nothing. The subtext of such a query is that words are tokens of things that are real, and are thus self-evidently true of the things they represent. (Contrariwise, 'speaking in tongues' is intentionally devoid of meaning, in order to express divine truth untrammelled by sense.) To ask why it thunders, Aristotle goes on, is to make a different assumption, not just to assert the existence of thunder, but its occurrence as a manifestation of something else. So 'thunder' is both a name and a definition, and its explanation 'a continuous demonstration', i.e. its expression as a (momentary) demonstration of processes that are true all the time (though Barnes suggests it to mean 'probably, "a demonstration that has immediate premisses" ', observing that 'Aristotle's illustrative definitions do not contain any *explicit* references to causation' (Barnes in Aristotle 1994: 224–5)).

The same thing may hold both for some purpose and from necessity. If something may be the case in this way, may things also come about thus? E.g. if it thunders because when the fire is extinguished it is necessary for it to sizzle and make a noise, and also (if the Pythagoreans are right) for the purpose of threatening the denizens of Tartarus in order to make them afraid. [94b] (Aristotle 1994: 59)

Aristotle jokes at the expense of the Pythagoreans, who encoded their esoteric knowledge of the mathematical and philosophical implications of acoustical processes in numerological mnemonics intended to baffle non-initiates. His thesis is that in the way the world is described we can distinguish different kinds of knowledge. Different kinds of knowledge are none the less knowledge for being different, but they are different by virtue of the fact that they are known and expressed in different forms. He examines the forms and relates them to the kinds of knowledge they express. Whether knowledge is true is not important; the fact that it is generally held to be knowledge is taken as evidence of its being true in some sense. Since knowledge is transmitted acoustically as well as in writing, and in geometric diagrams and arrangements of pebbles or abacus counters as well as in words, music by this definition is also knowledge of a kind.

Aristotle goes on to remark that certain kinds of knowledge relate to permanent features of the environment, and others to momentary events, and yet others to intermittent events. The way in which a particular item of knowledge is formulated tells us what kind of knowledge it is supposed to be. However, it does not follow that the knowledge is true by virtue of being articulated in a particular way. That Aristotle avoids discussing causation, incidentally, is because language in his thesis is not proof, but evidence of knowledge, and knowledge is evidence, not proof, of the real existence of underlying principles. Evidence, he remarks, is evidence of something, which is as much as to say that a mistake is evidence of error, and false witness evidence of perjury. The crucial point is that the 'primitive' sensory data giving rise to language are necessarily true of themselves because not only is language predicated by common experience but because the forms of language say something verifiable about the nature of the experience, and thereby of the events that give rise to it. This too has musical implications.

He is only too aware of the imprecision of words, and the fallibility of human witness. But imperfect though evidence may be, it is nevertheless a token of real behaviour and real experience, out of which it can be said that real knowledge arises. It is a sterile exercise to subject Aristotle's case-history formulations to legal scrutiny, which is to attribute a degree of absolute truth to language that was neither intended nor believed to be literally true.

As in theory, so in fact. Along with books, I have a varied collection of music: miniature scores, full scores, tapes, cassettes, LPs, and CDs. If I want to listen to music, there is a radio in the parlour, television, a cassette machine, turntable, CD player, and decent amplifier and speakers. I also have a memory for the music I like. Fragments of music come to mind at unexpected times: a classic blues currently serving as accompaniment to an advertising campaign for stone-washed jeans, or a famous aria from a famous opera whose name I forget, conveying the promise of escape to the good life courtesy of a certain airline. Abbreviated and musically incomplete though they are, these casual fragments nevertheless highlight a totality of experience, of the composition in question as much as of its associated mood, a totality moreover of place, culture, and time. But where is the music in reality? Does it exist other than as a transaction between a transmitting agent and a listener's powers of recall?

No collection of music exists as sound. We do not require music to be constantly audible. Indeed, we have no way of verifying the existence of a piece of music as an acoustic event. All that we can verify is a mental process arising from the modulation of an acoustic field in pitch, timbre, and intensity. Music is only audible as a temporal process, and the intersection of music and time is such that at a given instant only a moment in transition is available to hearing. Nevertheless, it is perceived as a continuum. Music offers no external equivalent to the 'freeze-frame' of video, a picture, or a book. Sounds emerge into being and fade into memory, and the totality of a musical performance resembles a kind of multi-dimensional mental map.

Our experience of music, nevertheless, is of something definite, not of a meaningless and ungraspable turbulence. Music impresses itself on to a temporal plane of which one co-ordinate is frequency, and the other a human time-scale of information processing and subjective experience. Objectively, time is unstoppable; in practice, it is processed and packaged into quantifiable units. Looking at the flow of water in a rippling brook, it is not possible to see that movement as a sequence of momentary states. It all happens too fast. Drop a leaf on the surface and the movement becomes intelligible. In music the movement of the leaf is melody, and the quantum of flow the beat. The time-scale of musical pitch is several orders of magnitude finer than the time-scale of conscious apprehension, which is why music can paradoxically be perceived both as instantaneous and as continuous. Where brain function is upset, the two perceptions can become confused, like the patient of Dr Sacks who showed remarkable persistence in his efforts [to write], and they were, initially, crowned with success. Unfortunately, his physiological disturbances made this increasingly difficult: he would either read too fast to take in what he read, or get stuck or transfixed on a single letter or word; his handwriting, similarly, would tend either to 'stickiness' and micrographia, or, more commonly, to be broken up into a multitude of impulsive jabbing strokes, which once he had started he could not control. (Sacks 1973: 100)

The world of acoustic perception is one of which the sounds of music provide a vocabulary of terms, and the concert repertoire a database of instantiated experiences. A trained musician can read a score and hear the orchestra play, or the vocal line sing, in the mind's ear. In the act of choosing which recorded version of a composition to play, a listener is making a judgement among memories of different interpretations, sound quality, and production values. From experience, a composer can imagine a chord and how it would sound played by this or that musical instrument. Nobody would argue that the notes on paper of a musical score are images of actual sounds. One wonders by what power of association it may be possible to identify music with a pattern of magnetic charge on a tape, or the miniature slalom of an LP track, or the digital information minutely imprinted on a CD. The sound and character of music is not embodied in a musical instrument, in the way the character of a poem could be said to be embodied in language. A musical instrument is like a blank page. It has to be articulated by a mediator, a musician. And it requires a memory of something to play.

The traditional response to impermanence as a condition of experience has been that of seeing the world in terms of isolated essential features and eliminating local or non-essential variables from the picture. The real world of experience then assumes an anecdotal relationship to the depicted essential or ideal world, just as in a musical or dramatic performance the individual personality of an interpreter is construed as incidental to the underlying text, and only rarely as part of its essential meaning.

2

Pitch

Bernard Dudot, Renault Sport's engine designer, once explained the complex process by which one [Formula 1] team worked out how many revs per minute another team's engine achieved. It entailed making a recording of the rival car at maximum speed and comparing its frequency to the frequency of his own engine.

(David Tremayne, *Independent on Sunday*, No. 273, 1995)

MOTORWAY cruising speed in my ageing Volkswagen is a comfortable 80 m.p.h. That at least is what the speedometer reads, though I suspect the reading is on the optimistic side. What I do know for sure is that at the speed giving an 80 m.p.h. reading on my speedometer, the engine is making a sound of a particular pitch, and for reasons partly to do with a training in music and partly with natural perception, I recognize that pitch as the note F below middle C. The note is a by-product of engine motion. Parts rotate, the rotations are revolutions (or revs), the revs produce a cyclical waveform, and the waveform is associated with a pitch of specific fundamental frequency (hertz, or cycles per second). A four-cylinder engine fires four times per rotation, each cylinder firing in sequence. What I hear as a constant pitch is a composite of four superimposed cycles of cylinder motion peaking at successive quarter-turns of each full cycle. The constant pitch is an indicator not just of the car moving at a constant speed, but also of the four cylinders firing in regular alternation.

It is an old car, and it has only four forward gears, and listening to the change in pitch that comes from changing down from top to third, or up from first to second, I can hear that the change in pitch is in simple musical intervals. For example, the pitch rises an octave if I change down from top to second, and rises another octave again when I change down from second to first; when I change down from third to second it rises by a fifth, and by a fourth if I change down from top to third. As the car is usually slowing down or accelerating at times of changing gear, the engine note is ordinarily in gliding mode, continuously rising or falling in pitch, so in order to arrive at an accurate judgement of the real pitch change associated with a change of gear ratio it is advisable to make a controlled test driving at a constant speed off the main highway.

From listening to the pitch of the engine in the various gears it is a simple matter to discover that the gear ratios from first to top are in simple numerical relationship. By musical coincidence the changes in engine pitch from first to top correspond to the intervals, or frequency ratios, separating the first four harmonics in a harmonic series: octave, fifth, and fourth. The gear ratios responsible are in inverse proportion to the pitch ratios, meaning that when the speed of travel is constant, a higher pitch means the engine is turning over faster to maintain speed in gear. Of course, the reason for having gears in the first place is to allow the engine to work efficiently across a range of possible speeds, so as not to stall at a standing start, nor overheat at top speed. A choice of gears also means that the engine can operate efficiently and economically within only a limited range of rev speeds: in my case, corresponding to a span of about an octave. We therefore work out that the gear ratios for this particular make and model of car have been selected to give a second gear of half the size, a third gear of one-third the size, and a top gearwheel of one-fourth the size of the gearwheel for first gear.

A Tour de France cyclist would have little use for a machine with only four gears. Seventeen, twenty-one, or more ratios are available to the human engine to cope with subtle differences in road conditions. This is because the human engine powering the cycle turns over at a much lower frequency, in the order of 2–3 hertz, compared to the engine of a car; the greater number of gears is designed to compensate for that human limitation of range. If one could hear the range of a cyclist's gear changes as pitch changes, the Tour de France would be a richly musical event, given the variety and subtlety of melodic intervals available to a system offering so many gear options. Unfortunately, this is a music neither cyclist nor spectator is able to hear, since for human ears pitch is an effect of cyclical processes in the real world oscillating within a range of frequencies between 30 and 4,000 hertz, equivalent to the seven-octave pitch range of a piano keyboard. Cyclic processes producing continuous waveforms in this (admittedly generous) range of discernible pitches can be monitored as dynamic events in themselves, and also as indicators of environmental conditions, and of the health of the individual.

The point of the story is to illustrate that looking and listening are different ways of coming to terms with reality, of negotiating with the world. One might even say that the world revealed to listening and the world revealed to sight are sufficiently different to be plausibly described as alternative realities. At the present time for most cultures the dominant representation of reality is visual. For most drivers a glance at the dial is sufficient to tell them whether they are exceeding the speed limit. That is all they need to know. And for a majority, the world is a visual reality which we consult and know about by looking and reading objects as sources of information. To a majority the idea of listening to the sound of a car engine as a means of gauging its speed may seem wilfully perverse. I do it because I learned music, and for my own amusement. But the fact that I can hear and interpret the engine note in the way described means that I am able to understand certain things about the car that a person relying only on the dial reading would not be able to register. So a listener has access to a different kind of knowledge, a knowledge invisible to the person in the driver's seat. The value of such knowledge, of learning to listen, is that it makes transparent aspects of the visual world that are normally opaque. That knowledge is musical knowledge.

One can go on to compare the reliability of acoustic compared to visual information. Confidence in estimating the car's speed at 80 m.p.h. rests on whether the source of information addressed is reliable in itself, and beyond that whether the information has any larger validity. From reading the pointer that says '80 m.p.h.' in front of me on the dashboard, I have no way of knowing for sure that the car is actually travelling at that speed. Sitting on rollers in a service station, it may not be moving forward at all. The truth of the dial information depends on an association between engine revs and wheel revs, and is subject in any case to calibration error. The driver simply cannot know for sure how fast a car is being driven by reading a dial. And of course, the information gained from a speedometer is only about speed, and about nothing else.

There is something right about [Hilary] Putnam's claim that the referent of 'electric charge' is fixed by pointing to the needle of a galvanometer and saying that 'electric charge' is the name of the physical magnitude responsible for its deflection. But, depite the amount that Putnam and Kripke have written on the subject, it is by no means clear what is right about their intuition. . . . Pointing to a galvanometer needle while supplying the name of the cause of its deflection attaches the name only to the cause of that particular deflection (or perhaps to an unspecified subset of galvanometer deflections). It supplies no information at all about the many other sorts of events to which the name 'electric charge' also unambiguously refers. (Kuhn 1993: 535)

Whereas I would not swear to be speeding at 80 m.p.h. on the evidence of the dial on my own car, I could very positively affirm that at the moment indicating 80 m.p.h. my car engine was turning over at the pitch F below middle C, a frequency of about 170 hertz. That corresponds to 170 impulses per second, divided by four for a four-cylinder engine, giving a rev count of (× 60) around 2,550 r.p.m. I have no use for that knowledge, but an engineer could use the information to verify how fast the car was actually going. Pitch is an objective measure of rotational speed, whereas the speedometer is not. Equally, my knowledge of the car's gear ratios based on the pitch changes related to gear changes, is knowledge that otherwise would only be available to someone who was able to take the car apart and measure up the various gears. By listening to the sound of the engine, one is able to assess features of its performance in action that a non-listener would have to dismantle the engine to discover. Having dismantled the engine, however, one would no longer be in a position to verify its behaviour directly.

Acoustic information is more than that too, since it is information about ratios and relationships that are universally true of vibrating systems. If I sing the intervals corresponding to the various gear changes, the frequencies and ratios coming out of my vocal mechanism are the same as those produced by the car engine. Furthermore, in this example the ratios are what a musician recognizes as simple harmonic ratios, which have a special significance, not only for music, but for how we understand the world around us.

Absolute pitch, enabling a listener to recognize frequencies and frequency ratios in real-life sounds and tones, is a musical gift but not a mysterious or occult power. Hearing involves a mechanism in the inner ear that distributes the sound as a spectrum of frequencies from low to high, much in the way that a prism displays light as a spectrum of colours. Dedicated arrays of nerve sensors react correspondingly to intensities of stimulus across the spectrum of audio frequencies in much the same way as the rods and cones in the eye are selectively stimulated to varying degrees by the colours of the rainbow. A sensation of colour is properly described as a characteristic pattern of peaks and troughs, and a sensation of tone and tone quality arises in a similar way, from the particular pattern of stimulation that registers across the audible spectrum. Normal human hearing partakes in that basic sorting and distribution mechanism of acoustic assessment: it is on such consistencies of physical make-up that communication relies. Absolute pitch, or something very like it, can be learned. An infant learns to identify its mother's voice; a professional musician can also acquire an absolute sense of the pitch to which an instrument is tuned. Acquired recognition of this kind amounts to an ability to 'read' the ear's response to pitch information, and thereby address specific zones in the neural array of the inner ear that correspond to particular pitches or frequency bands.

Such knowledge is useful, in the practical sense of making life simpler, and also scientific, because the information acquired is true and universal. There is much more to an awareness of pitch than party tricks. For normal purposes recognition of a particular sound as being of a particular pitch does not have to involve a notion of pitch, but only a sense of location in the auditory mechanism. Absolute pitch requires a code of absolute frequency to which a sense of pitch can be related, and absolute frequency in a modern sense is a time-dependent concept. In order for me to identify F below middle C as 170 cycles per second, there has to be agreement on a standard unit of a second of time, historically a recent development. Alternatively, pitch can be standardized as wavelength, a more ancient concept that survives in the description of organ pipes as 4-foot, 8-foot, 16-foot, etc. For most of us, however, pitch is not absolute but relative, and for determining relationships rather than absolute values. Without absolute pitch I would still know the gear ratios on my car, even if I were unable to tell exactly what frequency corresponded to the engine note at the time.

Tones of relatively constant pitch have self-evident value, and it is because they are specially useful across a range of practical applications that instruments of constant pitch play so prominent a role in the music of all cultures. Steady tones tell a listener that the world is a dynamic place. Not just that something in the world that is emitting a tone is thereby in motion, but that the environment is also in motion by virtue of that one continuous event. It is quite simple. My neighbour's electric hedge-clipper whines at a steady pitch. In order to be perceived as having pitch, the event must have duration on a microsecond scale, and for its pitch to be perceived as continuous, it must have duration on a macrosecond scale. It follows that the listener exists as a continuous being by inference of the sound being perceived as constant, and that the environment also exists as a medium of transmission and amplification of the sound perceived. (This is of some consequence given the difficulties in philosophy of establishing the objective reality of events in continuous time.) Pitch is detection of cyclical motion in the range of 30–4,000 turns or repetitions every second. Duration is a subjective measure relating the nature and persistence of the stimulus to a dual time-scale, micro-time or virtual instantaneity of pitch perception, and macro-time or response time.

A sound of constant pitch establishes an association with a specific region in the physical ear. As long as it remains constant the relationship it signifies remains stable. Monitoring a sound for pitch is an effort; monitoring a constant sound for change is a great deal easier. If a sound does not change it can be ignored, and indeed contributes to becoming ignored by habituation and eventual fatigue of the synapses affected. For a combination of reasons, lack of new information in the signal and falling-off of response of the appropriate nerves, we find ourselves switching off to steady continuous tones in the environment, and turning our focus of attention to other pitch regions.

In real life, few sounds are truly of constant pitch. Those that are, tend to be mechanical in origin. Machines that are made for use will vary in pitch and tone quality as a consequence of what is being done with them. A chain-saw lopping dead branches changes noticeably in pitch as it gradually overcomes the thickness and resistance of the wood. As a car meets an uphill rise or a dip in the road, the engine tone falls or rises according to the greater or lesser effort involved to maintain a constant speed. The corollary of a loss of hearing due to continuous exposure to static sounds in the environment seems to be a heightened sensitivity to any sudden variation in tone that may arise in these same frequency regions. A change in pitch or timbre means a change in the environment, and a change in the environment is something to which a listener needs to be alert as potentially life-threatening. Changes in reference pitch are of two main kinds, and they provoke different classes of response. Major changes, continuous or catastrophic, affecting pitch or amplitude, represented by the examples of changing from top to third gear, or a sudden interruption of continuity, as at the moment of sawing through a log, involve a redefinition of reality and the observer's relationship to it (not the least aspect of which is the restoration of normal hearing). Minor fluctuations or deviations in tone, not necessarily affecting the pitch, but perceived as low-level disturbances of quality, loudness, or smoothness, are more typically perceived as adjustments or realignments of a reality that continues unabated, and are therefore interpreted as events in a continuing relationship. Whereas large-scale changes are typically associated with dynamic features of the world beyond hearing, small-scale changes 'within the sound' are typically perceived as symptoms of functional changes in the signalling process, relating to the mechanism's fitness to continue functioning, or by assimilation, to functional changes in the hearing of the individual listener that may be symptomatic of an analogous physical deterioration in health. The sound of a light plane flying overhead produces a large-scale effect of change in terms of a pleasant, leisurely descending tone that gradually fades away, a change that is perceived as a normal effect of movement in space; the same sound, however, if heard to vary erratically in pitch, or occasionally to sputter or cut out, is perceived as signalling a malfunction of some kind, on the part either of the aircraft or the pilot.

In music, as in life, perceptions of constancy—that is, pitch,—and of consistent features within large-scale continuous processes in the audible environment—like the sound of a plane overhead or of a steady underlying harmony—are readily interpreted as corresponding to situations that are under some form of control. Equally, small-scale deviations from continuity, from the wavering pitch heard as the dentist's drill works its way round a tooth cavity, to the sob in the voice of an operatic tenor, are all significant or symbolic of dynamic uncertainty or loss of control. In music of every age and kind it is possible to identify areas that are constant in dynamic opposition to areas that are subject to potentially exploitable variation in a metaphor of the continuing balancing act of human behaviour. Western music has its gear changes, corresponding in magnitude and effect to the chord changes that carry a melody forward, and they can be used in a formal way, for example to define a narrative structure of verse, middle eight, and chorus. Chord changes themselves may be orthodox or strange, but they are nevertheless perceived as purposeful and ultimately objective. On the other hand, music also has its terms of individual expression, translating as a range of introduced small-scale distortions or modifications of tuning, of rhythm, of melody etc., that are perceived as outside the normal terms of reference and predictable course of a musical experience. These small-scale events are perceived as personal, are unexpected, and produce an uncertainty of response in the listener. An uncertain response is an emotional response: emotional first because we the audience don't know what's going on precisely and feel a groundswell of alarm; and second because (for instance, in the case of a song) a story is being told, and instability in the delivery of a vocal line can signify an emotional involvement in the events of the story. In the case of a purely instrumental number, emotional reactions can be triggered by a line of music that a skilled player can quiver, bend, accentuate, hesitate over, wail, waver, or choke to suggest an entire range of emotions.

There is a third locus of change, and that is in ourselves. As moving beings in a changeable environment, we influence and alter the balance of audible events by our own actions. Looking up when the telephone rings produces a violent shift in audible location of the source of sound, though we don't perceive it as violent because it is in balance with the action of looking up. There are subtle changes of tone quality that occur as a result of turning in the direction of a particular sound, arising from differences in the balance of response registering on our two ears. Such subtleties inform us of a sound's distance and direction. But in order to register as external events, or as changes in environmental perspective, sounds have to be assessed first as calibration signals for hearing itself, and for personal orientation, large-scale change against evidence of subjective physical movement (is the sound moving or am I?) and small-scale change against evidence of subjective failure of perception (is that a buzzing in my head or in my ear?). All that we hear is evidence that we are able to hear, and has first to be interpreted in terms of our continuing ability to hear. In using steady tones as references by which to build up an image of the acoustic environment, we are also using them to identify ourselves as stable functioning individuals.

3

Discriminations

Once we understand how the features that are characteristic
of living beings have a biological explanation, it no longer
seems mysterious to us that matter should be alive. I think
that exactly similar considerations should apply to our discussion of consciousness. The way, in short, to dispel the mystery is to understand the processes. We do not yet fully
understand the processes.

(Searle 1984: 23–4)

IF Descartes had driven a Volvo, he might have conceived reality
in dynamic terms. Driving a car relies on assumptions. I drive,
therefore I am, but don't ask to know where exactly I am, because
there isn't time to reflect, and besides, that isn't the point.

Philosophers, theologians, and scientists tend to be selective in their
choice of reality. Theirs is by preference a static world. It allows them
time to reflect. It is composed, ordered, reliable from one instant to
the next. According to Chomsky the choice of reality is appropriate.
'It makes sense to postulate mental representations in, say, the study of
language and understanding of language, or in interpretation of visual
space, but it is not appropriate to postulate them in the study of how
one learns to ride a bicycle' (Chomsky 1984: 2). Gilbert Ryle rode to
college on a bicycle, but he didn't allow that to interfere with his view
of reality. One can understand why. A world in motion is only nego-
tiable in approximate terms. It relies to a great extent on instinct. A
dynamic world is highly unpredictable. It relies to a great extent on
strategies of damage limitation. The accent is on survival, not truth;
moving around obstacles, not ignoring them. We are asked to believe
that being transported, whether by bicycle or by Beethoven, is not
congenial to serious reflection on the mind and its works.

Philosophers have long been in love with the quintessentially static image of the real world as a writing desk. Reaching for an example of everyday perception on which to construct a criticism of introspection, Wolfgang Köhler looks up from his paper and declares:

If I say that before me on my desk I see a book, the criticism will be raised that nobody can see a book. (Köhler 1959: 42)

On the formation of neural pathways, he says:

The thing we have before us on the table is called a book, and its parts, pages. It is a serious pathological symptom if someone cannot recall these names when the objects are before him as visual facts. (Ibid. 66)

Discussing order in the visual field, he remarks:

On the desk before me I find quite a number of circumscribed units or things: a piece of paper, a pencil, an eraser, a cigarette, and so forth. (Ibid. 81)

On the experience of events as exhibiting organized relationships in a unified external space, he observes:

The pencil on my desk is nearer to the book than to the lamp; the knife lies between the book and the fountain pen, etc. (Ibid. 123)

The desk image is a sacred tradition and a crippling intellectual liability, symptomatic of a narrow, medieval, bookish conception of reality. A. J. Ayer's *Philosophy in the Twentieth Century*, a guide to the thoughts of Bertrand Russell, G. E. Moore, C. I. Lewis, Karl Popper, Wittgenstein, and many others, returns to the nature of reality as a constant refrain, and every time discussion turns to mundane or even ultimate certainties the author glances at his desk for reassurance. Popper's thesis is flawed, the reader learns, because a cat is sitting on Ayer's writing desk (Ayer 1984: 134). C. I. Lewis's hypothetical reality of alpha-particles is countered by an appeal to the common-sense world of Ayer's 'objects like desks and fountain pens, which . . . fall within the boundaries of experience' (ibid. 88). Wittgenstein is caught wondering what is to prevent him 'from supposing that this table either vanishes or alters its shape and

colour when no one is observing it' (ibid. 156). And yet, in referring their arguments and the reader to the desk before them and the
various articles that lie on it, Köhler, Ayer, and all the rest are trans-
parently shifting their focus of attention from an interior imaginary
world to a mundane exterior actuality, while asking the reader to
believe that the two worlds are at the same time distinct and also
continuous. If the purpose of the desk analogy is to reinforce the
basis of reality of the imaginary world, then a reader would expect
evidence of a continuity between the two, and that is plainly not
the case. In order to philosophize about the real world, the philosopher has to create an imaginary world, and in order to verify his
imaginary world, he has to wake up for a moment and peer out of
the mind's window. There are not one, but two worlds: an internal orderly conception destined to account for everything, and a
messy external experiential world of spatially distributed objects.

Most of the centuries-long discussion about science and religion has taken
place in [a] middle ground where the complex relationship between facts
and their interpretation still keeps philosophers busy. Only the most
unphilosophically minded scientists now suppose that pure and simple facts
can be known to us outside a framework of interpretation, which is itself
the product of a long history. Take [Richard Dawkins's] comments on 'the
big bang of modern cosmology' and 'the myth of Genesis'. 'There is only
an utterly trivial resemblance between the sophisticated, esoteric conceptions of modern physics, and the creation myths of the Babylonians and the
Jews that we have inherited.' In a superficial sense that is true. . . . But once
we take the trouble to look beneath the surface and ask how these two
accounts have historically influenced one another, a more complex story
emerges. Many of the early cosmologists appealed to the Bible as the
source of their belief that there was an intelligible order to be found in the
universe. Likewise theologians, forced to recognize that Genesis could not
be interpreted as if it were a scientific account, began to see that its origins
lay, not in some kind of quasi-scientific speculation, but in historical
experience. (Habgood 1993: 59)

The 1992 Edinburgh Science Festival encounter between the
Archbishop of York and Richard Dawkins on the relative merits of
two very different creation myths is an interesting illustration of an
opposition created by the loss of an intellectual middle ground. In

this case, the middle ground is an understanding of the part played by musical acoustics in the conceptualization of creation. Dawkins challenges the theologians to demonstrate that the myths of religion, and the creation myth in particular, are able to rival the sophisticated and esoteric conceptions of modern physics, declaring that the myths of religion are incommensurate with modern knowledge, and deploring the language and pronouncements of theology as both counter-productive to healthy intellectual growth, and unworthy of serious debate. Dr Habgood for his part defends the creation myth and other myths of received religion as answering a continuing human need to believe in an orderly, intelligible universe, but he goes on to equate a continuing human need to believe in something with a continuing need to uphold historical precedent, even if what is being upheld no longer makes any sense. Early cosmologists, he implies, not only shared in the ordinary human need to believe in an intelligible universe, but had a professional interest in declaring the universe to be intelligible. The biblical account sanctioned that belief. One always starts from the supposition that the object of study is intelligible. (Which is surely Dawkins's point, that theologians should defend themselves more credibly, since, in the real world of scientific research, if you can't make a case, you don't get the funds.)

Forced to recognize that Genesis could not be interpreted as if it were a scientific account, theologians changed their defence of the creation myth as ancient science to a defence of 'historical experience'. However, as the early cosmologists were theologians too, and just as interested in developing a credible account of creation, any ensuing rift between cosmology and theology would seem to indicate that the cosmologists, as practical theologians, were prepared to adjust their beliefs to an expanding body of evidence, whereas their theoretical colleagues were not.

What is missing from the modern debate is a sense of the past. Both kinds of argument are essentially scriptural, defending opposing accounts of what constitutes a credible view of reality. But those scriptural accounts ultimately derive from an aural conception of creation. The biblical account no longer satisfies because it has lost touch with its origins in acoustic observations; the scientific account is insufficient because it ignores the contribution of hearing altogether. In accordance with his own view of Darwinian rationalism, Dawkins bases his challenge on an interpretation of the biblical creation myth as literally true: the account in Genesis is an account of the origins of the universe and the natural world. But an account of the creation as an act of will is by definition not a literal account of objective creation, but an account of what it means to arrive at a conception of the world as an objective reality. As such, it is capable of rational interpretation.

The objective world, as Piaget noticed, is not a given but an intellectual construct. Infants do not initially distinguish (or rather, do not appear to articulate a distinction, which is not quite the same thing) between themselves and a world of sense impressions. Even the most esoteric of philosophers argues whether there is a real connection between the language of sense impressions and the world of shared experience. The biblical creation myth can be—as I think it should be—understood as describing a dawning of consciousness, and not a coming into being of matter. It is creation in the sense of coming to terms with sensory experience and adaptation to the idea arising therefrom of an objective creation. The biblical account is everywhere *invoked*: at every stage of creation what is, is declared to be, which means that it exists in our consciousness by virtue of being declared, just as Newton is poetically elevated to existence by divine fiat: 'God said, Let Newton be: and all was light'. That is not the same as saying that the world was created spontaneously out of nothing. It is cleverer than that, and more up to date. It is even possible to read the Genesis account of creation as a birth experience: impressions of darkness, and movement across waters giving way to a revelation of light, and the contrast of light and darkness, and a new experience of the world as populated, extensive, and variable to the touch. In distinguishing the sky, seas, and land as habitations of bird, fish, and animal life, the creation myth is identifying primary sensory distinctions (wind, wave, soil, and stone) as features of a real environment with corresponding tactile and auditory associations of feather, fur, carapace, and scale, and of birdsong, animal cries, buzzing insects, and the slap of freshly netted fish. It is a story of creation as a process of increasingly focused distinctions and associations, and emphatically not an inventory of newly imagined products to stock the shelves of a supermarket reality.

The real challenge is whether we can truly say that a diverse creation exists prior to the mind arriving at an awareness of its distinctions. In identifying the making of distinctions as the creative act, the creation myth is being rational and consistent. There are also the consequences of the act of creation as a declaration of a distinction between the (divine) self and the world; these consequences include a loss of direct control over the world, and delegation of authority for maintenance of a stable creation, with the possibility of an original conception of order deteriorating into chaos, as events go their own way.

That leaves the question of accounting for creation as a divine act. It is divine not by virtue of being a one-off historical event, in the manner of the Big Bang, but by virtue of being consistent with all human experience, which implies that the individual experience of coming to terms with creation is not unique, but in line with the experience and accounts of older generations, and of generations to come. The most powerful way of declaring that consistency in experience is by representing individual experience as objectively guided.

Perception is mental activity arising from the interaction of the environment and the senses. The environment includes other people and their conversation as well as light and shade, heat and cold. The mental activity that gives rise to perceptions of the world is not so much something that we choose to do, as behaviour forced upon us that we gradually learn to control. We are obliged to perceive because we cannot prevent our senses from responding to everyday stimuli. Though everybody has the same senses, not everyone has the same perceptions. Senses are what you are born with, whereas perception is something you learn, a skill at interpreting sense responses that is developed and refined as one grows. As we live, so we respond to stimuli. Patients in coma on life-support systems are tested to discover whether they are capable of responding to light, touch, or sound stimuli of the most basic kind.

If they fail to respond to a series of tests they may be diagnosed as brain-dead. In conducting such tests, one is not looking for intelligent or correct responses to questions of fact, but reactions such as a blink, or a change of pulse.

For ordinary people, being brain-dead is not an option. They take consciousness for granted. They pass the response test. The proof of being alive and conscious is that people are responding to stimuli in the environment all the time. In fact, they do it rather well, so well indeed that the world around us appears more benign, neutral, factual even, than stimulating. Yet stimuli are fundamentally disturbing. They have to be, to do their job. If the world were not a stimulating place, we would not be aware of it. Since we are aware of the world, not only as existing but as changing, there must be something about awareness in general that is keeping the mind in a state of constant excitation.

The contemporary equivalent of Köhler sitting at his writing desk is you or I watching television, which is a graphic reality entered via a screen from which we periodically retire into our domestic reality in order to visit the bathroom or make a cup of tea. But television is dangerous. Unlike the written word, it can suffer brainstorms. The world of the writing desk is permanent and serene. Nothing changes. It is orderly, functional, and utterly reliable, as befits a rational conception of the world. Television by comparison is dynamic and emotional.

When I first bought a television set, nothing seemed to go right. I connected the aerial, and switched it on, and wherever I turned on every channel there was nothing but 'snow' and noise: no visuals, no voices, no music. I took the set back to the shop. Patiently the salesman showed me how, in order to receive an intelligible signal, I had to tune each channel to a different waveband. I took the set back home and found that after a few simple adjustments what had previously been an insoluble problem of chaotic reception was transformed into a coherent system defining a structure of choice among clear and intelligible programmes.

The same analogy can be used to distinguish sensory activity of a primordial kind, when the senses are switched on, from perceptual activity that is a consequence of deliberate tuning of individual responses. A television set is an electronic sensorium designed to respond selectively to the broadcast environment. Chaotic imagery of 'snow' and noise is the equipment's spontaneous response to being stimulated into action by electric power. A biologist might describe such inchoate stimulation as the equivalent of pain, since the information given out by an untuned television receiver in response to being switched on is unintelligible and without programme content. At this most fundamental level of consciousness, however, even incoherent snow and noise are information of a sort, demonstrating namely that the vision thing (to coin a phrase) and the sound system are actively functioning. A dark screen and no sound would lead one to conclude, after checking the power supply, that the set was indeed brain-dead, not that there was no sound or vision signal to pick up. The rationale of a television set can only be understood in relation to a context of receivable programme material, just as a telephone is only meaningful to a user in relation to other telephones and the possibilities of transmitting and receiving messages.

Despite their lack of programme content, unmodulated snow and noise are perfectly adequate signals for adjusting brightness and loudness levels. Sound and vision, brightness and loudness, are system responses that can be satisfactorily tested without the need for intellectual coherence—perhaps rather more satisfactorily, since there is nothing in the signal to distract the viewer. A feature of autistic behaviour is the treatment of other people's actions and attempts to communicate as the equivalent of noise on the line.

Imagine that ordinary human senses work in a similar way, operating at the most basic level as detectors of unstructured, unprocessed, or 'pre-processed' information that serves to stimulate responses telling us more about the senses' own activity levels than about the world at large. The advantage of such a model of sensory organization is that it accounts for the experience and at the same time for the fact that the experience cannot be satisfactorily articulated. We can describe the experience of such 'pre-processed' information as stressful, since it corresponds to sensory input that the subjective tuning mechanism cannot adequately handle, at levels of intensity that nevertheless demand some form of immediate response. The great advantage of describing basic human sensory responses as responses to disturbing or distressing stimuli is that the definition provides a motivation for the individual to respond defensively, 'without thinking', and only gradually learning to evaluate the stimulus and respond with a degree of self-awareness. Learning becomes a conscious manipulation of a process of reaction that arises from involuntary beginnings. In response to glare, eyes pucker up; in response to excessive heat or cold, the touch withdraws. Our interest is the shaping of auditory responses: how environmental sounds present themselves, and how they are interpreted. We are looking for a 'tuning' structure in human behaviour out of which a conscious awareness of the environment may be shown to arise.

The sensory feedback of everyday life doesn't come to us in neat packages and bite-size chunks. In order to convert unstructured environmental information into meaningful imagery, a television set has to be manipulated intelligently, and it is the same for human beings learning to perceive the world. Tuning a television set is a form of exploratory activity designed to examine the equipment's response over a range of broadcast frequencies. It can be random 'channel hopping'—pushing buttons on a handset—or methodical scanning across the spectrum of wavelengths. Either way, success is achieved when visual chaos and noise, or an unstructured continuum of images, give way spontaneously or momentarily to recognizable coherence. We recognize coherence in a signal by its relative stability. A signal that is relatively stable is easier to process. It requires less effort to register. In consequence, it is less disturbing. Eventually the viewer arrives at a procedural set-up that allows instantaneous access, with a minimum of signal interference, to any desired programme. We learn to perceive in a similar way, by a mixture of chance initiatives and strategic exploration of visual, aural, and other sensory fields, until the process of adjustment is so automatic we begin to regard it as natural, and to regard those who fail to attain it as underachievers.

Perception in television terms can be regarded as simple pre-programming. After all, most television sets are housebound. They don't move. Their sensory environment is also relatively stable.

Different channels have fixed wavelengths. But human beings aren't like that. People are naturally explorers. The environment that registers on the senses is constantly in flux. We like it that way. It keeps us happy and alert. It means, however, that human perceptions cannot be reduced entirely to preset responses. Because human nature leads us into ever new situations, and because the world accessible to human senses is thus by definition as well as by nature unpredictable, human perceptual activity can never entirely abandon its primitive exploratory character. That restless urge is matched by compensating strategies of self-protection from unwanted disturbance. In time those strategies can be deployed creatively to serve other purposes. Language, for instance. In reducing the possibility of mutual misunderstanding, language increases the possibility of mutual co-operation. Creating comfortable environments is another. In constructing temperature-controlled and acoustically protected environments to which people can escape and find conditions of visual and aural repose, we also create the possibility of structured learning and acoustic experiences (drama, music concerts) in which whole sections of a community may participate on equal terms. At the end of the day, when we have had enough stimulation, we hide in bed, in the dark, in order to sleep—though even these places of comfort and privacy can be further exploited for creative intimacies.

I want to present a certain 'naturalistic' view about the contents of the physical world—a view about what (physical) *things* (or *objects*) the world contains. This view may be crudely characterized by the mysterious-sounding claim that, in a certain sense, *there are no things*, but, partly as a consequence, there are as many things as we like. . . . Instead, [the world] consists of 'stuff' spread more or less unevenly and more or less densely around space-time. . . . I am taking it as a fundamental ontological doctrine that the raw material of the physical universe is *stuff*, not *things*, and that the organization of (some or all of) this stuff into things is done by *us*. I will not . . . attempt to define the term 'stuff'. I will not have anything to say about the *physical* nature of stuff, nor will I take a position on how many different kinds of stuff there are. (Jubien 1993: 1–2)

All realities are virtual, and some are more virtual than others. What we have here is a representation of the world of experience that is reachable from virtual reality technology or sound recording. The argument from visual reality expresses the world as pixels on a mental screen. We view the world, but what we see is actually a high-definition raster of points of light of different colours, as in a Seurat painting. Images on the screen correspond to things in real life, but everything seen consists of the same 'stuff', pixels. We ask why images are seen, and not points of different-coloured light. If a spot of red in one location in the visual field can be moved to any other location by a simple move of the head, and for that reason is potentially everywhere, why do we see it as being there and not anywhere else? And if the 'stuff' of pixel images is undifferentiated physically, there is no basis for differentiating one 'thing' from any other *on the evidence as it is presented*. Organization of the visual field becomes a matter of personal choice. This is novel. Instead of a world of conventional objects, things on a table, we have a conception that accounts for background on the same terms as things. Thingness is no longer a property of objects, but a property of decision-making. Perception becomes a form of 'action at a distance'.

Fortunately the analogy holds. The back of the eye can be compared to a miniature screen. The spot of red is here rather than there in the visual field because the lens of the eye brings the spot of red to focus at a specific point, and the resulting discharges from the rods and cones located at that point are themselves mapped on to a particular site in the mental representation. Fixed images are constructed out of an amorphous matrix by the brain applying fuzzy logic to a continuously fluctuating input. Without some form of processing the visual field would be a dizzying incoherence. Through a new pair of glasses one experiences the world afresh as constantly moving; making the world stop moving when the eyes move is something the brain has to learn. Even virtual reality headsets take some adjusting to.

As a description of auditory perception the notion of a world consisting of undelineated lumps of 'stuff' is relatively congenial. A microphone also doesn't differentiate. Sounds all around are connected by a continuum of air, flowing and combining in a complex pattern of pressure fluctuation. That fluctuating line visualized on the oscilloscope is an image of Wittgenstein's 'all that is the case'. (But if you want a world in stereo, then you need two lines, one for each ear, at which point even the great philosopher will admit that 'all that is the case' is neither one line nor the other, but rather the difference between them.) Acoustic stuff is received in an undistributed state: object location is the consequence of mental trigonometry on the basis of phase and intensity differences between inputs to the two ears. Audio frequencies extend over a far greater range of sensibility than light frequencies, from the largest low-frequency pressure fluctuations, sounds that are felt more than heard, up through the speech and music octaves to the smallest high-frequency vibrations beyond the limits of pitch and audible only qualitatively as image definition or brightness.

Another feature that connects Jubien's 'stuff' with acoustic space is its avoidance of considerations of defining limits. In hearing, this is normal. Few individuals before Gerard Hoffnung and Saul Steinberg have given serious thought to what shape a sound may be imagined to have: for Köhler, the word *takete* is an angular shape, and *maluma* a rounded shape (Köhler 1959: 133–4). In computer graphics a sound such as a pistol shot, for example, can be visualized as a mountain peak sloping away to a continuous background level where environmental reflections intermingle. But even that image is only true of a single point in space and time occupied by a microphone. The thing about sound is that from somewhere else the same sound is always different.

A sound in time is generally finite, having a beginning or onset, a more or less gradual decline, and in between perceivable qualities representing stable attributes that, in the case of musical sounds, are generally harmonic. Most sounds evolve in the course of time, in pitch, timbre, intensity, position, or a combination of these. A sound can be short or long, high or low, hard or soft. But it does not have shape, even though artists from the cave painters of Lascaux via Dürer and Bosch to Miró and Paul Klee have sought to depict real and imaginary soundscapes as surreal bestiaries floating in mid-air. Nor is the waveform much of a guide. An oscilloscope trace of an orchestra contains no clue to the presence of a flute or cor anglais. In sound there are no edges, only thresholds.

No engineer can determine for sure where one sound ends and another begins, either in space or time. Nevertheless sounds are differentiated, they can be located, and they can be analysed by you and me, simply by listening.

4

Consciousness

A heavily pregnant woman lies on a couch in an antenatal clinic while the theme tune from the soap opera *Neighbours* is relayed to her unborn baby though a speaker taped to her abdomen. As it plays, every movement the baby makes and its heart rate are monitored by ultrasound. Research was carried out on 70 women at Belfast's Royal Maternity Hospital, half of whom regularly watch *Neighbours*. When the theme was relayed to the foetuses of the soap's watchers, they became significantly more active. But when an unfamiliar tune was played to them, or the *Neighbours* theme was played to foetuses who had not been previously exposed to it, there was no such response. 'This shows foetuses of this age have a memory and can recognise familiar tunes,' Professor Hopper said.

(' "Neighbours" theme learned in the womb', *The Independent on Sunday*, 16 January 1994)

B ABIES can hear, are stimulated by, and respond to sound before birth. They develop in an environment transmitting the sounds of the mother's voice, her breathing, and heartbeat rhythms. In this 1993 study, near-term babies exposed to reproduced music were discovered to be more active in response to the theme music of a soap opera that the mothers routinely listened to than when alternative music was playing. The melody of *Neighbours* is a particularly astute choice: a hummable tune in the octave range below middle C. This is a frequency range that transmits readily within the body cavity, and a melody that can be sung or hummed without unduly tensing the diaphragm or straining the vocal cords, considerations important to women whose voice range is already lowered and mellowed by the experience of pregnancy. Having a loudspeaker taped to one's abdomen means that the music is transmitted by a direct but unorthodox route, a way of reproducing a standardized 'hum' for the unborn infant, without the mother having to sing along.

The evidence of heightened activity among the unborn subjects is taken to mean that the unborn child already has a memory. What is of interest to musicians is the unspoken corollary that in order to have a memory, the unborn child must also have a developed sense of hearing. That hearing is developed before birth has implications for the acquisition of language after birth, because the quality and range of frequencies audible within and outside the womb are significantly different. Whatever memory and associations arise from acoustic experiences inside the womb are going to be limited to a particular range of frequencies.

Among nuclear physicists it is axiomatic that the reality you observe at an atomic level is modified by the observer as well as the apparatus of observation. It makes sense to suppose that what an infant is capable of hearing is also influenced by the acoustic environment and the sensitivity of the ear. Let us see. The womb is a liquid environment surrounded by sound-absorbent tissue. The range of frequencies able to penetrate the mother's body and be detected by the infant ear is limited to the low and midrange, and excludes high frequencies. In the womb there is no echo. Other than as a tinnitus-like by-product of auditory nerve activity, the unborn infant has no experience of high-frequency sound, so can develop no memory of it. (Babies exposed to ultrasound scanning are supposed to experience a tickling sensation and not hear a sound.) The external sound world of speech and song will appear to the unborn as resembling the sound world of the clinically deaf, with its characteristically flat vowels and absence of sibilants. The impaired word definition of deaf speech, resulting from an inability to hear and therefore reproduce the high-frequency speech elements that give distinction to vowel sounds and consonants, has powerful emotional associations for normal hearing adults, suggesting mental disability, a blocked and tongue-tied personality, and one whose world of sensation and expression is lacking in variety. These are the intuitive connotations of a high-frequency deprived sound world, and to many people such connotations are emotionally disturbing.

Because of the limited range of acoustic information accessible to the unborn, any mental formation associated with hearing in the womb is going to be based on acoustic pattern perception within a band of frequencies significantly less than the ear is designed to process. Lack of exposure to high frequencies suggests a reciprocally heightened sensitivity to acoustic information in the upper range of hearing from the moment of birth. Something like the emotional effect of this rush of high frequencies is conveyed in the first-movement fugue of Bartók's *Music for Strings, Percussion and Celesta* when after a long introduction for strings the mutes are suddenly removed and the music breaks free from a shadowy sound world of restless violins and violas hitherto confined to their dark lower melodic range, revealing an upper register of piercingly bright and resinous string tone. We know that the ear is more sensitive to higher than to lower frequencies, and that sensitivity to high frequencies is linked to the perception and conceptualization of exterior space.

As it happens, human hearing is not uniformly efficient across the range of audible frequencies. From 40 to about 4,000 hertz (corresponding to the range of notes on the piano) we are able to identify sounds of stable frequency as specific pitches; above that threshold, however, the ear continues to be sensitive over a further two-octave band of frequencies (up to around 16 kilohertz), but is unable to distinguish pitches in this upper range. The neurological explanation for this lack of discrimination is that higher-frequency waveforms exceed the response threshold of individual auditory nerves. But then, life in the womb does not give the infant auditory mechanism any opportunity to gain experience of frequencies greater than 4,000 hertz, even though it is a more than adequate environment for monitoring fundamental frequencies (the tune, that is, not the speech content) in the range of the theme from *Neighbours* (around 100–330 hertz). There is something more than just coincidence in the fact that the frequency borderland dividing the world of musical pitches and the world of incidental noise, and additionally separating the subjective emotional world of vowel sounds from the objective articulate world of consonants, corresponds so precisely to the difference between hearing inside the comfort of the womb and the sound world of the high-frequency acoustic environment into which the newborn infant is thrust unprepared.

It is not only that these higher frequencies are a new experience, but also that they stimulate hearing in the region of greatest sensitivity. Superimposed on the comforting low tones associated with life in the womb, the newborn encounters a harsh continuum of noise in the high-frequency domain, noise not only highly distracting but highly responsive to every move of the unwilling listener. To the infant high-frequency sound signifies space and direction, an external world heard in stereo and perceived in terms of subtle phase and amplitude differences between signals reaching left and right ears. Babies not only hear acutely in the range above 4,000 hertz, but as parents will testify, emit powerful distress signals at very high frequencies, often virtually inaudible to adult listeners.

'High fundamental frequency appears to be a feature to which infants attend preferentially, and it is frequently a feature of child directed speech' (Gleason 1993: 147). The special function of high frequencies appears not to be fully appreciated by all audiologists, nor indeed by linguistics specialists, who traditionally attach a higher significance to vowels than consonants. This may in part be accounted for by a historical tradition of working with audiometry equipment of limited frequency range, from the simple stethoscope of medical science to the more specialized phonautograph of Léon Scott, the Graham Bell cylinder phonograph of the 1880s, and Rousselot's 1906 kymograph, a development of the cylinder phonograph, of which

the drum, acting as a low-pass filter, fails to pick up the higher harmonics of the sounds of the word. The resulting curve brings out at most the first and second harmonics. A kymograph tracing therefore does not suffice to analyse the distinctive sounds of the words (its phonemes), but it is good enough to study the three prosodic parameters, duration, intensity, and pitch. (Léon and Martin 1972: 31)

The kymograph remained in use as a tool of language research right into the age of the tape recorder, its limitations actively defended by many as allowing the researcher to focus on the significant features of speech (namely vowels and intonation) without the distracting interference of consonantal noise.

Intellectual attraction to the midrange of speech and song may also be linked to a nineteenth-century romantic interest in the psychology of vocal melody as a medium of emotional expression. The development of cylinder recording coincided, after all, with the development of Freudian psychoanalysis. Ballantyne consistently identifies the most important frequencies for the perception of music and of speech as lying within the range up to 4–5 kilohertz, within which temporal coding (pitch discrimination) plays a major role. While acknowledging the dependence of speech intelligibility on consonants, she is only concerned to define the latter in somewhat negative terms: 'Frequency discrimination deteriorates abruptly above 4–5 kHz, the upper limits at which temporal coding is possible' (Ballantyne 1990: 47–9). Deterioration is a curiously loaded term for what surely, in a region of greatest aural sensitivity, is logically a transition to an alternative evolutionary function. The continuing disproportionate focus on vowels and speech melody is especially surprising today given the wealth of evidence that their contribution to speech intelligibility is actually less than that of consonants.

Although consonant sounds generally have lower average intensity, they contribute more to speech intelligibility than do vowels. There are several ways in which this can be demonstrated. One way is to eliminate the amplitude extremes of a speech waveform by means of a modifying device. Since the vowels have the largest intensity, with this process their intensity is reduced more than that of consonants. This procedure produces virtually no decrement in intelligibility. On the other hand, if the center of the speech waveform, that part containing the low intensity speech sounds (consonants) is eliminated and the extremes retained, speech is rendered unintelligible. (Small 1978: 168)

That lower average intensity is nevertheless spread over a much broader frequency bandwidth. It is noteworthy that in the literature of sonagram analysis of speech, the sound spectrograph records of speech patterns are normally restricted to a cut-off point of 5,000 hertz, the upper limit for vowel discrimination, though far from being the upper limit of consonantal sound. The effect of restricting sonagram images of both consonants and vowels to a sub-5,000 hertz bandwidth may have been inadvertently to reinforce the view that little information of any value is conveyed at higher frequencies. On rare occasions where an image is reproduced that extends above the 5,000 hertz ceiling, the visual impact of consonantal energy is striking. A demonstration sonagram of the syllables [si] and [ki] extending to 11,000 hertz shows unexpected prominence of high-frequency energy in the two consonants (Potter *et al.* 1966: 304–5).

The importance of high frequencies for transmitting spatial information is well understood by architectural acousticians. High frequencies are rather like lasers, in that they are extremely directional, can be beamed in straight lines, are absorbed by soft furnishings and reflected off hard surfaces, and reveal the presence of obstacles by the acoustic 'shadows' objects cast in their path. High frequencies register on the ear more rapidly, because of their more rapid rise time, and even though they last only for a brief instant in the onset of a musical tone, are retained as the defining impressions of the special tonal character of many instruments, including brass, keyboards, percussion, and plucked strings such as harp and guitar. (For proof one has only to play back tape recordings of instrumental sounds in reverse: the piano sounds like a harmonium with a terminal kick to every note, the trumpet like a flute, etc.) High-frequency signals such as parental 'tsk, tsk' and kissing noises, baby rattles, and the clatter of cutlery are excellent sources of environmental information for infant and adult alike, having the multiple advantages of alerting attention, signalling location, and provoking room response. Making noises in this range is a trick babies quickly learn for themselves. They are encouraged to do so by the provision of jingles, rattles, bells, wooden toys, and hard reflective surfaces for percussion play.

Orthodox study of acquisition of language in infancy, and of the language deficit in the case of autistic children, also starts from the view that language is necessary for thought, and that consequently the answer to how a first language is acquired is the answer to how human beings acquire a capacity for thought. It is an enormously tempting objective. Leaving aside individual differences of approach, the objective defines its own terms of success. It is focused on language, and on the point in child development where language coherence in adult terms is achieved (bearing in mind that infantile language is also an adult definition of language). The transition process implicit in the term 'acquisition of language' implies a goal of language communication that is simultaneously a goal of coherent self-expression. The acquisition of a skill implies a prior absence. What remains to be addressed is to what purpose infants vocalize in advance of language. The question of intermediate stages of vocalization having alternative goals, and developing other concepts and skills, is one that language study ought to address but does not. The idea that language in infancy is qualitatively different from adult language, and that infants have qualitatively different thought processes that transform by evolutionary stages into adult thought processes, is hardly satisfactory. Why should prior processes necessarily be discarded as new processes are acquired? Surely speech can perform a range of different functions simultaneously. Since speech also involves manipulating and monitoring acoustic events, some if not all of those functions are bound to continue into adult life.

Emphasis on language as a holy grail distracts attention from the mastery of more basic life skills, such as riding a horse, self-defence, and acquiring habits of courtesy to others (to pursue the Arthurian analogy). Alternatively, language, and language-related infant behaviour, can be interpreted as elements of an acoustic signalling and monitoring process of a more fundamental kind. For that, other criteria are needed. The evolutionary goal of this process is self-orientation. It involves making sounds, influencing sounds, and monitoring sounds. Acquiring vocalization skills is only part of the programme. Other voices and other sounds and incidental noises in the environment play an equally important role. We consider not only the implications of active mimicry and articulation, but also the implications of listening, balance, and the effects of voluntary and involuntary movement on auditory perception. In such a context infant vocalization is seen to differ from other noise data primarily in that it is capable of being modified by experience eventually to achieve specific results. Language is the trade-off of acquisition of the skills that make language possible.

Infant listeners monitor their own vocalizing. To oral cultures the larynx, as the source of sound, is the centre of individual being, the voice filling the throat, mouth, and nasal cavities. Language is traditionally conterminous with 'tongue', the organ both of taste and food consumption (taking in of material sustenance) and of speech (probing the environment and 'ex-pressing' spiritual being). Most listeners are initially alienated by the sound of their own voice on tape. It is an unfamiliar image. Equally, most listeners learn to ignore the sound of their own speaking voice. Doing so is a feature of self-confidence. Attention to the sound of one's own voice is normally a sign of a disabling self-consciousness. In acoustical terms the reflected environmental image of a person's voice (that is, the image as others and the tape recorder hear it) is substantially obscured by internally transmitted sound travelling directly to the inner ears.

We hear the sound of our own voices by two routes, one the usual air con-duction route and the other by so-called bone conduction. In the latter, the skull itself is set into vibration and these vibrations are transmitted directly to the inner ear, by-passing the middle ear mechanism . . . Experiments have in fact shown that we do seem to hear our own voices at a higher level than would be perceived by a listener close by. This arrangement makes a good deal of sense . . . In the absence of a system which favours the hear-ing of one's own voice a bizarre situation would develop in which each singer [in a duo] would continually attempt to out-vocalize the other. (Hood 1977: 35)

The inward voice is special. It occupies a physiological and psy-chological 'inner space' located inside the head. That inner space has no lateral dimensions, no sense of left and right, since the voice frequencies conducted within the body radiate equally to left and right inner ears. (Singers recognize a 'vertical' dimension to the inward voice, however, distinguishing high 'head' tones from low 'chest' tones.) In addition, the inward voice coincides with the speech act, whereas the environmental voice reflected back to the speaker is delayed by the time required for the voice to radiate out into a room and be reflected back to the pinnae (outer ears). Infant monitoring of acoustic information has to contend from day one with the masking effect of the internal voice on the voice as it is transmitted and reflected atmospherically. The brain has to learn to subtract the internal voice from the reflected image, as astronomers subtract the images of bright stars in order to see more clearly features in the background of a photographic image. What is left is a peripheral, residual external world image consisting of high-frequency information and phase-delayed midrange frequencies. Since high frequencies occupy a microsecond waveband, they are ideal for monitoring the microsecond delays characteristic of normal room response. Stereo phase-delayed midrange frequencies also translate that spatial information into pitch ('phasing').

Learning to navigate in acoustic space can be done without making noises or vocalizing. One can opt simply to listen to what is going on. A vitally important means of controlling the sound environment is by movement that directly influences the direction from which a sound is heard to come. Continuous or intermittent sounds that stay in one place (such as kitchen noises in the next room, or a radio, provide useful acoustic beacons for infant ears. The ability to use sounds as positional beacons depends on a sampling and matching process of monitoring the phase information of the signal at different angles and distances. Having two ears is a significant advantage. Observing pattern in the acoustic environment is equally effective whether the source of information is intentional or involuntary.

Adult belief in the primacy of visual perception in infant development has led to other peculiarities in representation of aspects of hearing development. A striking example is the test of infant hearing involving making a noise behind and to the left or right, out of visual range, and evaluating the response. Invariably the child is said *to turn in the direction of the sound*:

By the age of 6 months a normal baby will sit up unsupported and therefore will be able to keep his head firmly in the vertical position. This makes it possible for the child to make full use of the orientation reflex which compels him to turn the head towards the source of a significant, sudden change in the environment. (Fisch 1987: 35)

This is a logical impossibility. The infant cannot intend to see something it cannot see, so the movement is not of the eyes 'towards the source', but of the affected ear 'away from the source'. Piaget makes the very point. An infant cannot intend the continued existence of something that is not seen one moment and then use that information to decide to turn in a particular direction in the next moment. What happens in fact is that the child responds to a sudden disturbance in the acoustic field and takes avoiding action. It is adults who interpret the avoiding action as action with visual intention. The appearance of avoiding action in a child that can only move its head is easy to misinterpret as action to bring the source of the disturbance within the field of view. The fact that avoiding action is almost bound to be expressed as turning to face the source of sound gives added credence to an error arising from an apparent bias in favour of interpreting behaviour as intentional and governed by visual priorities. Blind infants presumably respond in the same way, and nobody would suggest they were driven by an intention to see what was happening.

Avoiding action is a way of ameliorating distress by putting distance between the self and the apparent location of disturbance. Infants, however, cannot run away, so their avoidance strategies have to be based on containment and control. Actions having the effect of lessening the local intensity of an audible stimulus include head movement, which has the effect of softening the impact of a sound by spreading its location, and crying, which is not only for attracting attention but is the creation of an inner disturbance having the effect of masking unwanted exterior sound. When an infant turns in response to a sudden noise the 'smear effect' reduces the intensity of the noise, and only incidentally may allow the eyes to be brought into play. The action also has the more immediately useful consequence, for an infant whose visual discrimination is still only limited, of bringing both ears into play, and the disturbance potentially into balance, allowing a determination, as and when the sound is repeated, that the disturbance is real to both ears, and not merely a malfunction of the ear initially affected.

Symbolic avoiding actions persist in maturity. A person signalling 'no' by shaking the head laterally is effectively 'delocalizing'—smearing the location associated with a voice—from central and specific into the background, thus taking avoiding action in respect of the sound of the opinions and incidentally scrambling the visual image of the person who is the source of the sounds. A person signalling 'yes' by vigorously nodding up and down is creating a disturbance in the other person's visual field while effecting minimal disturbance of their own acoustic field. Ears are on the axis of the nodding action. This difference in effect is demonstrated by binaural recording. It is very disorientating to hear a binaural recording in which the acoustic field is scanned laterally, from left to right, much less disorientating if the movement is symmetrical, i.e. from the perspective of a person running. In the first case the entire field of awareness is set in motion, as on a roundabout, whereas in the latter case there is a symmetry of induced movement that continues to allow individual features of the acoustic field to be monitored against a background. (We are all like J. J. Gibson's pigeons in this respect.) So nodding 'no' is a gesture of wiping the auditory slate clean, whereas nodding 'yes' is a gesture of silent self-affirmation in a context of preserving necessary discriminations in the acoustic field.

Why self-affirmation? Because nodding 'no' or 'yes', or any spontaneous head movement produced in response to a sound stimulus or experienced as an effect of voluntary or involuntary exploration of an acoustic field, is at the same time a gesture capable of being construed as reinforcing an awareness of self as distinct from the environment. Just as the traditional image of school learning is of children having to sit still and pay attention, so intellectual development in infants is traditionally linked to a gradual mastery of posture, and of hand and eye co-ordination. But this is to ignore the achievement of co-ordination involved in the process of hearing itself. Learning to listen in infancy does not, indeed cannot require a prior mastery of basic disciplines of outward stillness and self-control: rather, it could be argued that the reverse is true, that it is primarily due to exposure to the acoustic effects of involuntary movement: being picked up and rotated in space by an adult handler, swaying unsteadily in a lap, being burped over a shoulder, and propelled at speed in a reclining position to an accompaniment of gruff voices and environmental noises from all directions (all of which experiences tend to make adults that suffer them feel quite nauseous)—that infants acquire the basic understanding of self in relation to others and the environment, on which all subsequent learning depends. Children retain a love of violent spatial experiences that adults find difficult to stomach. They are excited by violent movement in space. A sense of balance is associated with the middle ear; a sense of spatial location with high-frequency acoustic information. There is a connection between acquiring a sense of spatial orientation and monitoring high-frequency information. It is why children squeal with excitement on a roller-coaster.

That monitoring the acoustic environment does not require intention, or focusing on an object, or controlling the incidence of sounds in the environment, or an attitude of stillness, is enormously important. It frees the task of accounting for perceptual growth from the logical presumptions of in-built concepts of the self and the external world. Babies have initially to adjust to an acoustic world that is highly dynamic in ways they cannot control. Any head or body movement of an infant with functioning awareness of an audible background will produce a perceptible change in the phase and intensity information of the reference. Sighted adults no longer consciously notice these dynamic cues; the blind depend on them for finding their way round. From birth the infant is aware of a distinctly new region of auditory perception related to the outside world. What the infant has to learn is that acoustic movement in the environment is in reciprocal relationship to the individual action that causes the environment to move. That sense of reciprocity is the key to awareness of the self as separate from the environment. In becoming aware of the world as an environment in dynamic partnership with the self, a range of conventions are intuitively acquired: conventions underlying melody, rhythm, movement, the relation between sound and silence, and the spatial and emotional associations of different frequency regions. These buried conventions are what motivate adult listeners in their appreciation of music, which consists of abstracted and intensified patterns of environmental cues. All that is necessary for distinguishing the self from the world of external sense impressions is recognition of a connection between the quality of the movement and audible change. Interior sound disturbances do not change. Exterior sounds do.

5

Speech

> We can be deeply stirred by hearing the recitation of a poem
> in a language of which we understand no word; but if we are
> then told that the poem is gibberish and has no meaning, we
> shall consider that we have been deluded—this was no poem,
> it was merely an imitation of instrumental music.
>
> (Eliot 1963: 55)

T HE poet acknowledges the nonsense poems of Edward Lear, and
defers respectfully to the inspirational gifts of Mallarmé, but in this
context T. S. Eliot would appear to be alluding directly to the *Ur-
Sonate* by the Austrian *émigré* Kurt Schwitters, a composition for
reciter in abbreviated sonata-form. It is not an abstract *poem*; nor is
it a composition of sound effects like Marinetti's *Tzang-Tumb-
Tuuumb*, a futurist evocation of World War I trench warfare. Its
nearest equivalent is *musique concrète*: fragments of speech emptied
of verbal meaning and available afresh as phonemic music.

Before language comes speech. Speech is the noises human
beings make on the way to expressing themselves in language.
Language is that part of speech commonly understood as having
meaning. Speech has no need to be socially meaningful, though
there is a social dimension in simply making noises in order to be
noticed, which is an endearing quality human beings share with
free-range chickens. Speech can be perceptually meaningful without having to be socially meaningful. Then, you may say, it isn't
speech. I may agree, but it is still treated as such. 'From the earliest
months of life a child's caretaker will systematically respond to the
child's utterances as if these utterances were intentional . . . communicative intentions are evident before words are learnt'
(McShane 1980: 145). Perceptual meaningfulness has to do less

with words than with the information potential of vowels, consonants, and diphthongs, alone and in combination. That potential is
partly acoustic and partly gestural.

Language acquisition in infants assumes a process the aim of
which is the acquisition of language. Accordingly, pre-language
vocal behaviour is considered as intentionally or otherwise directed
toward mastering the techniques of consonant and vowel production, and acquiring the sense and use of a vocabulary. Speech is
understood as spoken language, i.e. written language in spoken
form. It attends primarily to language as information communication, the criterion of language acquisition being the successful
exchange of information. The adult's intention is both projected
on to the infant's behaviour, and is allowed to deflect attention
from any more 'primitive' purpose that may be adduced from the
actual sounds infants articulate and their acoustic effect in a domestic environment. Much the same tyranny of retrospection can be
found in the study of the development of writing skills. The traditional account of the history of writing is of an activity developed
with the sole aim of faithfully rendering the sound patterns of
ordinary speech. Such accounts, Olson observes,

suffer from what I take to be a critical flaw. They assume what they need
to explain. Specifically, they assume that the inventors of writing systems
already knew about language and its structure—words, phonemes and the
like, and progress came from finding ways to represent these structures
unambiguously . . . as if all attempts at writing, always and everywhere
were crude attempts at the transcription of the sound patterns of speech.
. . . Pre-writers had no such concepts. The development of a functional
way of communicating with visible marks was, simultaneously, a discovery of the representable structures of speech. (Olson 1994: 67–8)

In addition, the history of writing reveals inconsistencies in the idea
of what constitutes an adequate representation of speech, some
alphabets providing for consonants alone, others for consonants
and vowels, yet others (many of them influenced by language specialists, ITA for instance) introducing additional letter-forms to distinguish diphthongs and varieties of consonant. What is especially
striking is the primary importance of consonantal distinctions in the

history of writing, in view of the greater attention traditionally accorded to vowels in English language phonemics. The significance of consonants should be obvious, given that they so outnumber vowels in the alphabet.

Reversing the orthodox view, Olson proposes that writing, as a system of communication, actively influences the writer's perception and understanding of spoken language. That would seem to suggest that the meanings of words are similarly influenced by the sounds and associated physical actions of speech. There is certainly good recent evidence that phonetic discriminations have influenced music. Research into automatic speech recognition, translation, and synthesis was launched in the 1950s in the belief that speech could be reduced to a relatively small repertoire of phonemic units able to be assembled in different order to make any desired word. The same general idea inspired, among other works of the period, Stockhausen's 1955 electronic composition *Gesang der Jünglinge*: an idea planted in the composer's mind by Professor Werner Meyer-Eppler, in whose seminar the composer studied phonetics and information science.

Meyer-Eppler's researches at Bonn University were in turn part of a wider research effort, much of it government-funded, whose military goals included the development of devices for the automatic interception and transcription of radio and telephone communications, and among peacetime applications, provision of a computerized translation service for international bodies such as the United Nations. Experiments in dissection and reassembly of tape recorded speech elements quickly demonstrated that these objectives were not realizable. Speech was mistakenly imagined to organize itself in sound in discrete packages, as it appears in print. But continuous speech does not easily break down into easily identifiable and manageable segments. There are intermediate stages, transitional elements between syllables and between consonants and vowels, and further variables arising from the influence of speech elements on one another, from differences relating to language, and from those relating to the individual voice.

The core of the difficulty is the complex and variable way linguistic messages are encoded in speech . . . For a computer to 'know' a natural language, it must be provided with an explicit and precise characterization of the language . . . Although a capacity for understanding language may be the ultimate goal, the enterprise of speech recognition is really founded on the identification of words. (Levinson and Liberman 1981: 56–7)

What had originally been conceived as a simple mix and match operation slowed to a halt as the impossible vastness of the repertoire of available speech sounds became apparent. Among those to suffer was Noam Chomsky, whose influential 'deep structure' thesis was destined not to be implemented by computers monitoring international telephone calls but received a new lease of life as a brave new model of human language acquisition, at which stage it became necessary to appeal to genetic programming to justify its operational rationale and make it work.

As long as language is regarded as permutations effected on a limited set of speech elements, infant acquisition of language can be plausibly accounted for as an evolutionary trial and error process guided by environmental conditioning. The new perception of infant acquisition of language against a background of infinitely variable phonemic units made a trial and error thesis logically difficult to sustain. The alternative that suggested itself was a programmed 'universal grammar' directing a process of selection from a pre-existent repertoire of available language distinctions. Since the programme had to be universal, it would have to include distinctions proper to all languages. That is what Jean Berko Gleason appears to suggest by the word 'ability' in alluding to research indicating that

Canadian babies can distinguish the Czech [ř] from [ž], although Canadian adults are unable to hear the difference between these sounds (the first is a combination of [r] and [ž], as in the composer's name *Dvořak*, and the second is the sound [ž] as in the word *azure*). Thus, Werker and her colleagues have shown that infants from eight to ten months of age have the ability to discriminate phonemes that are not in the local language, whereas the adults in the community cannot. (Gleason 1993: 157)

There is just the merest suggestion here that infants are born with powers of language discrimination that are lost in the acquisition of a mother tongue, or in growing up, or both. It later emerges that Gleason's point has also to do with disposing of an alleged symmetry between language acquisition and progressive language loss in old age or as a result of deterioration of brain function. Thus it was Roman Jakobson who claimed that 'dissolution of language reproduces in inverse [*sic*] order the pattern of acquisition. Jakobson had noted that the Czech [ř], which is acquired last by Czech children (for good reason!) is also lost early by Czech aphasics' (Gleason 1993: 171).

To the Canadian infant, of course, the sound has nothing to do with a foreign language. Calling it a Czech [ř] is simply an adult way of giving the sound a name along with an entirely alien cultural baggage. Phonemes are merely sounds that those who specialize in language are motivated to identify as components of a language, and which they may not know how to describe in any other way (though other ways do exist, for example the graphic shorthand of 'visible speech' (Potter *et al.* 1966: 60–3)). Discrimination between phonemes is no different in essence from discrimination between other kinds of noise. Canadian adults unable to distinguish a Czech [ř] from a Czech [ž] are nevertheless able, one would assume, to tell the difference between the sounds of a teaspoon and of a fork falling to the floor. That the phonemes in question belong to any particular language is only relevant to language specialists. Acoustically, the distinction is unambiguous:

The [sh] and [zh] sounds are characterized by a wide band of fricative energy which, in steady state, extends from about 1,500 Hz to over 7,000 Hz. The energy in these sounds usually peaks at about 2,600 Hz. Thus, their invariant frequency characteristics are quite unlike . . . [s] and [z] (which) have most fricative energy at between 3,600 and 7,000 Hz and, due to antiresonances, relatively little immediately below the major peak. (Ling 1976: 272)

An approach that sees language acquisition as the main or only criterion in evaluating infant vocalization skills may be unable to understand the point of vocal abilities and utterances that have no apparent linguistic function. Liberman has suggested that in listening to speech for its language content, adults ignore major acoustic features and focus in on cues specific to the speech code (Dascal 1983: 64–5). Hence the description of speech sounds as 'Czech', and the implied specification of infant language as 'utterances that exhibit grammatical structure'.

The alternative question is how simple non-verbal acoustic distinctions are translated into concepts without passing into language. I have suggested that the basis of infant conceptualizing about the environment may be attributed to a division of hearing function (i.e. auditory processing) into frequency regions below and above the 4,000 hertz threshold. The lower is a region of specific pitch, of vocal and melodic intonation, of the piano keyboard, of vowel discrimination, of frequency control: it is the region of emotional expression; the range of frequencies above 4,000 hertz is associated with the complementary perceptions of indiscriminate pitch, noise, articulatory percussion, consonants, instrumental timbre distinctions and involuntary effects: this is the region of spatial awareness. We therefore look for indications of meaning in the phonemic structure of infant vocalizing that can be related to these frequency-related functional associations.

In answer to the question 'how do children learn to talk?' John McShane begins by declaring 'Words, *qua* words, do not have any salience for the child initially. "In the beginning was the word" is exactly wrong; in the beginning was the utterance' (McShane 1980: 1). One might assume the author to mean that an utterance has meaning as a sound, if not as a word. But this is not what he means at all. Quite the reverse. A child using the sound *mummy* in the context of requests from its mother cannot be said to mean 'mother' by the utterance since the sound alone does not correspond to a word with that meaning. For the sound to be accepted as a word meaning 'mother' it has to be used in combination with other words in a socially meaningful way. 'There are no more grounds for saying "mummy" represents the child's mother than there would be for saying "help" represents the child's mother' (McShane 1980: 2).

But indeed there are. The sound 'ma-ma' can be interpreted, as with 'pa-pa', as free vocalizations of infant feeding actions of which the meanings survive into adult life as 'mm-mm!' and 'puh!', terms respectively of appetite enthusiasm and visceral disgust. The lip-smacking action of 'mm-mm' is actually and metaphorically associated with suction and ingestion at the onset of feeding, just as the plosive 'puh' associates with satiety, rejection, and expulsion at the end of feeding. There are good reasons for saying that the action and sound of the utterance 'mummy' do indeed represent the child's mother, as a vocalization of feeding behaviour in which the mother is physically involved. 'At the sensorimotor stage of the child's mental development, "There is minimal or no gap between speech and thought. Speech is a new form of co-ordinated action, which, in sensorimotor intelligence, *is* thought"' (McNeill 1978: 187, cited in Dascal 1983: 67).

A television advertisement for Strongbow cider uses the image of a pair of arrows fired into the mahogany top of a bar. The evocative sound effect associated with the image and action of the arrows consists of a 'fzzz' onset to represent the arrow in flight, and a terminal 'thunk' representing the actual impact. I noticed that this same acoustic image of a sudden physical blow is expressed in a number of English monosyllables that range from the neutral via the impolite to the downright rude. These words begin with a diffuse consonant ([ff] [ss] [sh] [th] [h] etc.), passing by way of a short vowel to an abrupt terminal consonant such as [k] or [t]. Other more innocent words such as 'shoot', 'hit', 'fit', 'sick', 'shock', 'thud', and the demonstrative 'that' also follow the formula, and many carry a similar directional connotation. Since the starting consonants are indeterminate high-frequency noises that merge into frequency-specific vowel sounds, all of these words articulate movement in a downward pitch direction as well as processes of coming to focus at a definite point in space and time. Not all consonant-vowel recipes work equally well: 'thug' just might qualify, coincidentally (it is an Indian borrowing), but 'thick' and 'fog' make unlikely candidates for target practice.

Such acoustic images are more likely to be acknowledged in nonsense language than in educated acceptable speech. That also seems right, in that a great deal of normal speech has more to do with private acts of self-expression than with conveying sensible information to others. There are, for instance, a range of words ending in 'zzle', 'ssle', and equivalents. They are not rude or offensive, but more like pet words: fizzle, muzzle, nuzzle, sizzle, dazzle, frazzle, whistle, grizzle, puzzle, razzle, hassle, guzzle, tussle etc. We can describe these words as onset, short transitional vowel, and terminal 'zzle'. The distinguishing feature of the 'zzle' termination is excitation within the mouth, i.e. action that literally gives the speaker a buzz inside. Vowel pitch gives a sense of location to the buzz: [i] being 'more remote' than [a] which suggests something uncomfortably close, while [u] conveys a distinct impression of physical interiorness. Finally the initial consonants suggest a possible extended gamut of tactile associations. For instance:

m—mouth/taste (ingestion);
n—nose/smell;
p—lips/rejection;
d—eyes/face (saying [d] makes the face pucker up);
s—ears/external environment;
g—jaw/stomach;
f—skin/touch (irritation)

etc. So 'muzzle' and 'nuzzle' represent facial excitement, 'grizzle' and 'guzzle' stomach excitement, 'tussle' and 'puzzle' external sources of internal excitement, 'hassle' and 'frazzle' diffuse tactile sensations, 'fizzle' and 'sizzle' diffuse external irritations.

Vowels are location qualifiers by virtue of their locus of action in the mouth, as indicated by the mouth aperture and associated position of the tongue. These locations are recognized by audiologists: among English vowels [i] and [ɪ] are 'high-front', [e] 'mid-front', [æ] 'low-front'; [a] 'low-central', [u] and [ʊ] 'high-back', [ɔ] and [o] 'mid-back', and [ɑ] 'low-back'. In addition, vowels are determined by formant frequency relationships, vocal harmonics of voice tone. 'As the constriction produced by the tongue increases and moves towards the front of the mouth for the vowels [æ], [ɛ], [e], [ɪ], and [i], so are the lips slightly spread. As the tongue is elevated toward the back of the mouth for the vowels [a], [ɔ], [o], [ʊ] and [u], so are the lips increasingly rounded' (Ling 1976: 221). Recognition of these positions as virtual locations is taught by specialists to deaf children: in a therapeutic context they are given as real; and for infants and poets who employ such distinctions intuitively it is reasonable to imagine that vowels are also perceived to have spatial associations. The virtual location of a vowel is further influenced by its acoustic properties, namely how the vowel behaves as an acoustic signal in an enclosed or open environment. Whether we choose to shout hi, hey, ha, ho, or halloo in a given outdoor context will be determined by how the different 'carrier' vowels are perceived and used as acoustic signals. With distance the higher frequencies of speech are progressively attenuated by atmospheric absorption; lower frequencies on the other hand are also weakened, but in consequence of human hearing being progressively less sensitive to lower frequencies the farther away and fainter the voice. Vowel combinations can also be understood by the same token as expressing direction, for example the out-in vector of the expression 'hey-you' ([ei] is a front-of mouth diphthong whose second formant rises in pitch, implying movement 'out of the face', whereas [ou] is a back vowel implying a location 'in the face' signifying 'come here') in contrast to the in-out vector of the French 'holà' signifying 'go away'. (Or 'go away' itself, in fact.)

Infants acquire vowel discrimination indoors. The walled enclosure of a room actively helps the discrimination of vowels by selective feedback that at the same time allows the experimenting vocalist to discover the sound of a reflective space through the vowels best suited to provoke an audible response. 'Localisation of a sound in a resonant environment is especially acute between 2,000 and 5,000 hertz, where hearing is up to 3 dB more sensitive to the direct than to the diffuse sound' (Meyer 1978: 18). Vowels likely to benefit from this increased sensitivity are [æ], with a second formant peaking at about 2,320 hertz, [ɛ] at 2,610 hertz, [e] at 2,680 hertz, [ɪ] at 2,730 hertz, and [i] at 3,200 hertz (the last close enough in frequency, perhaps, to receive a further boost from the natural resonance of the ear canal of *c*.3,500 hertz).

Direct sound from a source in front of the listener and picked up equally by both ears is also uplifted around 3 dB in perceived amplitude in comparison to sounds heard from a source to either side. When the signal reaching both ears is balanced, the two inputs add up to a louder impression, but when the input is unbalanced, and one ear is receiving the majority of the signal, the onside signal tends to mask reception at the offside ear. There are probably good survival implications for this. Research by Kimura (1964), Spellacy (1970), and others further suggests that the left ear is more efficient than the right in processing melodic information (Damásio and Damásio 1977: 145–8), which may throw light on why string players from violinists to double-bassists place their instruments on their left rather than their right shoulder, favouring their left ear for listening to the instrument, and leaving the right ear free to monitor room response. I have a cutting from a British *Sunday Times* profile of the lutenist Julian Bream, illustrated by a photograph of the great man at an upright piano. His beaming face is turned toward the viewer, and unpianistically tilted so that his left ear is almost touching the keys, as if to pick up the vibrations inside the instrument as though it were a lute or guitar.

Vowel distinctions are especially enhanced in enclosed spaces. Before the Greeks learned to experiment with assisted resonances, they are likely to have observed, as children instinctively discover, that vowel sounds are great fun to shout in sacred places such as caves, canyons, and temples, and that the reflected sound changes in character as the initiating vowel is itself changed. And what children learn at play, senators and priests in conclave practice in earnest, in the music of ceremonial speech and the brave cadences of political rhetoric. The resonant theatres of religion and government demand a stylized mode of speech, one in which pitch levels have to be firmly and clearly articulated, for intelligibility of course, and equally for setting an appropriately solemn or emotional tone. Medieval congregations ignorant of Latin took their bearings from the vowel modulations of the Mass: the granite declension of [i] through [e] to [o] of the *Kyrie eleison, Christe eleison*, and the softer, more comfortable [a] and [u] of the *Agnus*. The music of vowels was familiar to troubadours and poets of the first Elizabethan age. To hear the 'Stabat iuxta Christi' by the fifteenth-century Eton composer John Browne is to appreciate the contribution of vowel coloration to emotional timbre. The verses oscillate back and forth between the Latin vowels [i] and [a], and in timbre between a dark woodwind sonority [i] and a brighter, brass-like radiance [a], the two characters resolving on the final 'gaudia':

Stabat iuxta Christi crucem
  Videns pati veram lucem
  Mater regis omnium
  .   .   .   .

Virgo mitis, virgo pia
  Spes reorum, vivis via
  Virgo plena gratia,
Iube natum et implora
  Servis tuis sine mora
  Nobis donet GAUDIA.

6

Doubt

To Professor Julius Bauer.
Dear Doctor,

I had meant to ask you about the following problem, but did not want to keep you longer than necessary.

It seems to me people should be trained to describe their pains correctly, since these are, after all, symptoms of disease. I, for instance, as you may have noticed, cannot do this, and I am convinced that I am not the only person of the kind.

Is a stabbing pain like being stabbed? A burning one as when one gets burnt? A drawing pain like being drawn, pulled? Etc.

What is a referred pain? What are colic, cramp, asthma, etc.? What is breathlessness?

It would perhaps be possible to establish a unified terminology and the relevant descriptions and definitions if one could begin by getting doctors to describe their own pains and then examined the general mode of sensation as reported in replies to questionnaires.

(Schoenberg 1964)

MUSIC comes under the rubric of deviant behaviour for two principal reasons. First, it plays on a listener's emotions, and second, it works in ways we cannot explain. Emotions are subversive, since they deny reason and lead to unaccountable behaviour; they are also resistant to rational enquiry. Music is like that. 'It needs no words. Because it needs no words, it is not amenable to normal thought processes' (Wing and Bentley 1966).

Remarks such as 'I see' or 'I hear what you are saying' use the language of sense awareness to make coded assessments of an intellectual kind. We take the remark 'I see' to mean 'I understand', and

'I hear what you say' to imply 'I understand but do not entirely agree'. Such coded responses are framed in language aimed, among other things, at persuading a listener that the response in question is based on direct perception and is therefore reliable. By maintaining the appearance of innocence, one avoids the pitfalls to which more robust observations are prey (for instance, a punch on the nose). It is easy to graduate from a practice of deprecating emotion in human affairs, to a doctrinaire exclusion of it and other 'irrational' behaviour from rational debate about a rational world. Informally, we continue to distinguish a 'naturally perceptive' individual from an educated intellectual by a characteristic quickness of judgement, attributed to 'sharp instincts' and 'good breeding', standing in contrast to the methodical thought processes of conventional wisdom. The fictional example of John Mortimer's Rumpole of the Bailey expresses the traditional understanding of wit as a human quality very different from what we understand by the received wisdom of the law. Quickness of perception, especially when set against the typical slowness of legal argument and the formality of court procedure, lends a certain credence to the view that perception is instantaneous and therefore innate, but for those very same reasons, not wholly reliable. There is a conflict of interest between sympathy and objectivity, between native intuition and ultimate truth.

Nevertheless, a doctrinaire exclusion of all such 'irrational' behaviour is itself profoundly irrational. 'The situations that we call painful or unpleasant are those in which we cannot fit the input of nerve-impulses to our set of rules,' remarked Professor J. Z. Young (Young 1960: 116). 'Since there is no fit we seek to make one by ascribing the disorder to some agent that we call the "pain" within us. . . . To describe any situation by saying that it gives pleasure, without further specification, is, as with "pain", a confession of failure to describe it in adequate detail.' And, echoing Wittgenstein, 'If the quality and nature of pleasure is by definition incapable of description, then it is also not a subject for verbal discussion' (ibid. 117–18). The viewpoint is unexceptional for 1950. It is current in 1984: 'Pains and other mental phenomena just are features of the brain (and perhaps the rest of the central nervous system)' (Searle

1984: 19). It carries a certain swagger. It also acknowledges certain limitations and values in relation to the essential subjectivities of all human knowledge, including how we come to know what it is we know, and whether we can ever be sure. The experience of relatively unstructured sense impressions is associated with infancy, autism, injury, illness, and the influence of drugs of various kinds. The trouble with such conditions is that they tend to inhibit effective communication—not surprisingly, because effective communication demands a prior ability to perceive the world objectively, itself a prior condition of using language—and when we emerge from these same conditions, as from a coma, we don't usually remember too well what the experience was like. It is doubtless for such reasons that science until recently tended to regard evidence from the very young, the ill, and those under the influence of mind-altering chemicals, as unreliable, and their experience of life as therefore diminished and inadequate.

As a Protestant Jew Spinoza was concerned to defend the rights of such minorities:

Since it is the supreme law of Nature that each individual thing endeavours, to the full extent of its power, to preserve itself as it is without regard to anything but itself, it follows that each individual thing has this sovereign right, namely, to exist and act just as it is determined by Nature. So far as this is concerned we acknowledge no difference between mankind and other individual natural identities; nor between men endowed with reason and those to whom true reason is unknown, nor between fools and mad-men, and sane men. Whatsoever an individual thing does by the laws of its nature it has a sovereign right to do, inasmuch as it acts as it was determined by Nature, and cannot act otherwise. (*Tractatus Theologico-Politicus*, XVI, 175, cited in Roth 1929: 125–6)

Nevertheless, the emancipation of 'unreason' has taken time. Freud legitimized first-hand accounts of dreams, presumably because his subjects were lucid and trustworthy in waking life. Neurologists have given qualified endorsement to the reported perceptions of patients suffering brain injury or symptoms of mental disorder, presumably because the victims' subjective observations could be said to be based on a foundation of previously normal behaviour and intelligence. Oliver Sacks's confidence in the testimony of victims of a chronic lethargy restored not only a reader's sense of their underlying lucidity but also their dignity as human beings. More recently Professor Young has returned to the subject of pain, and the view he expresses now is less magisterial. 'In studying pain we seem at first to be free of questions of reality: the pain is perceived by the sufferer as in himself; it is not some possibly questionable external object or event.' And yet, 'Pain does not follow a search for the answer to questions, as most perception does. It asks the question itself' (Young 1987: 102–4). That is a very different view, and it contains an important clue.

At least we know where to start. Whatever mechanism is involved in switching on consciousness has to involve the senses, the brain, and the environment. The task is to explain how consciousness can arise involuntarily, and how knowledge of the world can be achieved without prior intention. Suggestions that human beings are switched on to self-awareness and the rules of grammar by genetic programming, or as a result of excessive nurturing, are missing the point. The acquisition of language, which is interactive between persons, still leaves the question of individual consciousness unanswered. Consciousness arises from the interaction of the individual with the environment, an interaction that language use only partly addresses. 'Hearing is not only the first major sensory system that enables an infant to perceive signals from the outside world during intra-uterine life, but it is also the most important means by which a newborn baby can keep in contact with the environment for some time after birth' (Fisch 1987: 51). 'Hearing', *nota bene*, not 'speech': the world of sounds passively monitored, as well as sounds a new-born infant may utter voluntarily or involuntarily.

Interaction with the environment is revealed with awesome clarity in the behaviour of autistic children. 'Autism' is a drab term meaning 'selfhood' of a pathological kind. Its distinctive features are antisocial types of behaviour: in the use or absence of language, in the co-option of others into a private and highly formalized regime, and in a refusal to negotiate with one's peers or those in authority. For observers, explaining autism is a problem similar to the problem of explaining pain: first, in that there is evidence of suffering; second, in that there appears to be a connection between the suffering and an inability to communicate through the normal channels of social language and interaction; and third, that the suffering is contained through self-imposed regimentation of the personal environment and individual behaviour, affecting family and other people who are part of the personal environment.

The conclusion that autism expresses a mental deficit expresses much the same logic as the conclusion that pain expresses a mental deficit. That is, it cannot be real because there is no way of describing it. But that is to ignore the characteristic behaviour of autistic children, which on the contrary is highly suggestive of strategic responses to acoustic distress. The term 'autism' means a condition of being trapped in a world of one's own, and is identified with behaviour suggesting an abnormal intensity of individual responsibility for creating order in the world of one's perceptions.

I often watched [Toscanini] and finally realized at what point in his rehearsals the difficulties that were often associated with him began: it was only in works which he loved above all else. If he was rehearsing a Rossini overture, he simply played it through. As music it was so self-evident to him that the orchestra realized at once what he wanted. But when he rehearsed Debussy, for example, there were always the most almighty rows. I think he had a tonal image of *La Mer*, for example, which was simply not realizable . . . But the really major problems that Toscanini encountered at rehearsals always arose when Beethoven was on the programme . . . I know of one rehearsal in Vienna when Toscanini began to work through his usual repertoire of enraged reactions, throwing the score to the ground, smashing his watch and swearing at the orchestra. The [Vienna] Philharmonic players knew what was coming and were prepared for it. So that when Toscanini tried to go one better and abandon the rehearsal, he found that the orchestra had locked both the doors leading away from the platform. When he tried to get out of the hall and found himself standing in front of the locked doors, he realized that his outburst of anger had been anticipated. For a few minutes he went and stood in a corner, like a small child, and was ashamed of what he had done. He then returned to his music stand and wasted no more words on the situation, but continued with the rehearsal. (Karajan 1989: 78–9)

If an individual fails for whatever reason to recognize the reciprocal relationship between individual action and corresponding distortions of the acoustic and visual field, or cannot stay in control of the effects of action on the sensory environment, a state akin to panic may ensue. Persistent adualism (Piaget's term for childhood inability to perceive the world as anything other than an extension of the self) produces symptoms of primordial doubt. Among them are intensified evasion strategies: stillness and silence, exaggerated movement, self-injury (objective experience through pain), repetitive vocal and physical actions, and production of 'masking' continuous, high-intensity noise. Such behaviour is regarded as irrational, but it is more intelligible as a protracted (and by implication, unsuccessful) application of normal responses to painful disturbance, that is, rational strategies of self-reassurance brought on by an overwhelming impression that the perceived world, including other people, is too sensational to bear, strategies also predicated on awareness of the world as a self-created artefact. Panic arises because, despite that conviction, the world is nevertheless subject to change. Effects are not lasting, life goes on, and the terms of reference of normal experience are constantly having to be revised.

It may well be the case that an individual diagnosed as autistic may be suffering from a system defect in processing sensory information. What is more contentious is the degree of emphasis placed on a lack of apparent willingness to communicate, or to acknowledge the efforts of others to communicate, and the association of non-communicativeness with mental disability. Autistic behaviour is certainly asocial: to call it anti-social is to interpret a legitimate resistance to enforced socializing—whether by parents or by clinical psychologists—as deviant behaviour. The problem for observers of autistic behaviour is that they fail to perceive it as necessarily therapeutic, and see it only as destructive in terms that include carers as equals (or indeed, as superiors). The range of behaviours associated with autism can be more fairly understood as routine non-verbal, essentially pre-verbal strategies designed to recover a sense of order in an extended environment of ordinary perceptions. It is behaviour that has the effect of neutralizing the disturbing influence of others by reducing their active contribution to the individual's sensory input. The evidence lies in the behaviour itself, which can be related directly to infant strategies for making sense of a visual and aural world experienced as constantly in motion through the intervention of others.

Symptoms of autism relate to the normal processes of evasion of sensory distress which are part of the natural development of self-consciousness. Autistics exhibit as individuals many of the behavioural traits society finds acceptable in institutions of government and business: a rigid adherence to protocols, indifference to individual emotion and personality, reference to the self in the third person, and so on. Many of the stereotypies of autism are encountered in data processing and computer-related social behaviour, for instance relations with the bank or tax office. We have learned to handle such behaviour in society, and we certainly do not regard either the actions of a computer or of its servants as irrational, much as we may be irritated by them from time to time.

Many features of autistic behaviour are cultivated in the arts of dance, drama, mime, and music. There is more than a hint of echolalia in the incantatory repetitions of Gertrude Stein, of mantras, of prayers of penance, and the music of minimalist composers, and the incessant repetition of formulaic phrases arguably serves the same therapeutic purpose of clearing the head and focusing the mind. The performing arts involve individuals in creating an imaginary world. These arts are highly formal. They legitimize behaviour in which individuals either do not speak at all, communicating instead through gesture, through music, by mimicry, or, if speech is involved, by the stereotyped intonation of a memorized script. A recurrent feature of autism is an unexplained artistic gift, in music, in drawing, or in number-crunching. Clinical attitudes to such gifts appear to betray an apprehensiveness about individual talent and artistic expression *per se*. If autistics respond to situations beyond their control in the manner of prima donnas, then so equally do prima donnas. Are we deceiving ourselves in imagining there to be any real difference between Toscanini's temper tantrums and classic autistic behaviour? 'The difference is Toscanini.' But being Toscanini only means that other people are normally much more accommodating (unless the orchestra is having a bad day). Gillberg and Coleman express the hope that 'the enigma of the

beautiful child tip-toeing into your waiting room, gaze averted, is
beginning to yield to the diagnostic techniques of contemporary
science' (Gillberg and Coleman 1992: 8). So a child tiptoeing rather
than walking, and with accompanying arm- and wrist-flapping, is
defined as a clinical problem. But ballet dancers go round on points
and gesticulate gracefully with arms and hands. Dancing on points
is traditionally perceived as the behaviour of a spiritual being. That
'avoidance of direct gaze, toe-walking, a fixed stereotypical expression and handflapping' is characterized as a disability in children but
not in adults leads one to suspect that it is not so much because of
the activity, but because it is children who do it; perhaps, were they
trained in their movements as adults are trained, we might understand and appreciate more why they do it.

Symptoms of adualism persist in adult intellectual life.
Philosophical doubts about the correspondence between the inner
world of sense impressions and the real world of things may lack
pathological symptoms: after all, the individuals concerned are
trained, articulate, and professionally secure in themselves, and the
doubts they have about the verifiability of the real world are given
in terms of a shared experience, which is also a shared anxiety. But
the doubts are rational doubts.

Right now, the book is present in my experience. The question is: what
do we mean, that is, refer to, by 'my experience'?

One thing seems clear. We do not mean anything I can actually pick
out or focus on right now, in the way that I can focus on the book. When
the book is present in my experience, there is something of which I can
judge, '*This* is a book'; there is nothing of which I can judge, '*This* is my
experience.' By my experience we do not mean something that is, right
now, demonstratively available. Nor do we mean something that might
be demonstratively available. The argument is simple. Anything that is, or
might be, demonstratively available is something actually or potentially
present in my experience. But what is actually or potentially present *in* my
experience cannot *be* my experience.

This means that there is, in a sense, nothing which is my experience:
there is nothing (no object or process or event) in the world which is my
experience. The argument is as before. Any part of the world is potentially present in my experience. So no part of the world can be my experience. (Valberg 1992: 120–1)

It may be objected that philosophical doubt is at a level of sophistication far beyond what an infant or autistic child could conceivably attain, and therefore is less pathologically real. But that is to assume, once again, that language is necessary for concepts and concepts are necessarily verbal, and without the ability to verbalize autistic children do not have conceptual ability and therefore cannot be expected to experience doubts of a sophisticated kind. It is surely as logical for some individuals in the grip of primordial doubt to understand that the ultimate inadequacy of language is part of the problem. It would then be consistent in such a situation not to resort to language, since language does not provide an escape from the dilemma of being trapped in the bubble of one's own perceptions. Since language is ultimately no guarantee of objectivity, to use language to make the point is both self-contradictory and ultimately meaningless.

Musicians can readily identify with the behaviours of autism. Creating a self-contained and self-controlled environment by non-verbal means is what they do. If we are to deal effectively with autism then we must first of all divest clinical definitions of autistic behaviour of irrational negativism, always remembering that 'there is as yet no hard evidence that there exists a qualitatively unique behavioural or aetiological syndrome of autism' (Gillberg and Coleman 1992: 39).

A well-known undergraduate text, now in its fifth edition, describes autism as 'a pervasive developmental disorder' and diagnostic criteria as including a 'lack of awareness of others' existence, failure to seek comfort from others, failure to imitate others, abnormal or no social play, no developmentally appropriate form of communication, abnormal or no nonverbal communication, absence of imaginative activity [*sic*]', etc. (Bootzin and Acocella 1988: 451). It is almost as though a sense of personal affront and anxiety prevents the authors from accepting that individuals can prefer being alone, or be content in themselves, which is another way of characterizing 'inability to reciprocate, failure to treat humans as anything but objects, major problems in comprehension of mime, gesture and speech, little use of communication skills, delayed and impaired development of spoken language from ostensible lack of understanding to a rigid and extreme literalism, and immoderate behaviour that can be either hyperactive or seemingly lacking in initiative' (ibid. 451).

The common denominator of all autistic behaviours is hearing and the connection between the sensations of hearing and the image of an orderly world. The strategies of autism are auditory strategies, and they include what clinicians describe as 'seemingly non-communicative *echolalia*, avoidance of the personal pronoun, repetition parrot-fashion of entire conversations, repetitive asking of questions to which the answer is already known, and detailed recall of texts without evident understanding of, or concern to understand, their meaning. Autistic speech may be staccato, a continuous high-pitched monotone, or "scanning" (continuously moving in pitch)'. The speech of 'high-functioning' (able to hold a conversation) autistics is typically flat in tone and robotic in rhythm.

In auditory terms, all speech utterances and head movements have a subliminal self-referential function as well as an ostensibly social function. They influence the acoustic environment and can be evaluated as either reinforcing or modifying an existing mental image of the environment. An environment can be enclosed or an open space. In an open space, such as in a playing field, there is little local reflection of speech or noise: the sounds one hears are by and large those transmitted directly from sources at a distance: other children, passing cars, dogs barking, etc. Children shouting with glee on an open playing field will hear only the interior voice and a high-frequency residue, and that is why they run. Children running and wailing continuously are behaving as though to increase the pick-up of external sound residue by the pinnae by propelling themselves into the bubble of sound they are emitting. An enclosed space, by contrast, reflects sound, and it does so in a manner consistent with the acoustics of the room itself. Sound engineers clap inside a hall and listen for how long it takes the sound to decay, and for any peak in the reflected sound, a shimmer or twang of fixed pitch indicating an acoustic anomaly in construction. All children learn how to evaluate the sound of their environment, from the familiar noises of the kitchen and the bright acoustic of the bathroom's tiled walls to the less familiar or predictable enclosures of the supermarket, church, and museum. They learn by experiment, and the experimenting involves all the techniques favoured by autistics: intermittent and continuous sounds, monotone and gliding tones, tones at differentiated pitch levels, and repetition at specific frequencies. These techniques are the stuff of musical expression. In our enjoyment of music we project our needs for acoustic reassurance.

In acoustic assessment of the environment, the meaning of signals in language terms is not a criterion. In fact, communication can be perceived as a counter-productive distraction: first, because the demands of coherent speech interfere with the function of individual words or noises as acoustic signals; second, because talking sense provokes a response in others that is unwanted because it interferes with the signal being monitored; and third, because the response of others further complicates the situation by demanding a response from the individual already preoccupied with monitoring the room response of an initial signal. So the meaninglessness of autistic utterances in communicative terms has a positive aspect, an intelligent purpose matched by their function as auditory probes. We should learn from their example to take more care in matching utterances to their acoustic properties, because a propensity to emit signals in specific frequencies, intensities, and repetition rates can reveal what kind of information is being monitored, and for what perceptual reason.

Our culture is averse to suffering, which may be why the idea of sensory distress as a condition of living is hard to entertain. The Stoics taught that a painful existence was to be uncomplainingly endured, in contrast to the disciples of Epicurus, who believed in the pursuit of pleasure. We tend nowadays to think simplistically of the two as civil opposites, the Stoics as glum puritans, and the Epicureans as cavaliers; but both philosophies are more complex, and their complexity and subtlety rest on a concept of pain as somehow intrinsic to human nature. The pursuit of pleasure involves the avoidance of pain, and indeed pleasure in the Epicurean sense is also defined as 'peace of mind' or 'freedom from pain', which is far from representing a position of thoughtless hedonism.

In all kinds of pleasure what is experienced is one and the same thing, namely freedom from pain. Katastematic pleasure is the experience of the healthy functioning of the organism, in which that state is experienced as painless. But that state can also be experienced in another way, as one moves towards it, for example when by eating one gets rid of the pangs of hunger. In this case [according to Hossenfelder] what is felt is not, as on the traditional view, the special sensation of kinetic pleasure, caused by the process (*kinesis*) of return to the natural, that is painless, state. Rather, it is that state itself, experienced (apparently) to a greater or less degree the more or less closely one approaches it. (Taylor 1987: 243)

Hossenfelder's view attributes to Epicurus degrees of variation in painlessness, a view described by C. C. W. Taylor as 'incoherent': 'no quality can be absent to a greater or lesser degree' (ibid. 244). The criticism is that values cannot be assigned to degrees of absence, presumably because there is nothing to measure. However, there is a musical analogy, in consonance with painlessness, and degrees of pain with degrees of dissonance. The instrument with which these degrees are quantified is the monochord, and the existence and valuation of a hierarchy of consonances was a major preoccupation of that time. Epicurus is applying the principles of musical harmony to human sensations; there is thus a parallelism between a doctrine of the pursuit of pleasure and that of striving for harmony with the divine.

The implications go further. Just as a monochord has to be vibrating in order for its pitch to be determined, so the Epicurean perception of states of painlessness (or states of grace) presupposes a state of being 'in vibration' as it were in a continuum of sensation. It is this continuum of sensory stimulation to which the term 'pain' is assigned. Normal people don't experience pain as a condition of ordinary living. But if the term 'sensory distress' is substituted for 'pain', the idea of human activity being directed in some fundamental way by the need to avoid exposure to intense stimulation of any kind seems rather more plausible. The word 'pain' means only that a sensation is out of control. What Epicurus is saying is that as we shield our eyes from the glare, cover our faces against the rain and wind, block our ears against loud noise, steer clear of poisonous smells, and retreat from all things disturbing when we are ill, so the dynamics of human life are directed by avoidance of excessive and distressing stimulation. We may only notice extreme cases, but all sensation is distressing to some degree. In autism we may recognize patterns of behaviour that are strategies for coping with a hostile sensory environment. The alternative to a vegetative dependence on external stimuli to direct our lives is conscious recognition of their potentially malign influence and development of a life-style directed toward their control. The arts, including music, are models of sensory organization: that is why they give pleasure.

7

Naming Names

ASKED to tell the difference between one sound and another, a listener today may respond in a number of ways. One high-tech method involves reproducing the field of varying intensities of a sound sample as a contour landscape representing amplitude as height, and frequency and time as longitude and latitude. An alternative is the two-dimensional sonagraph or 'voice print' used in language research, forensic acoustics, and studies of birdsong, portraying the shape of a sound as an evolving smudge. Electrocardiogram reports deal in rhythm and line, expressing in visual terms activity that a stethoscope detects as the sound of the heartbeat; different medical conditions sampled at different points add up to characteristic patterns of frequency and amplitude, and combinations of waveform. Reading sounds in visual form is an acquired skill. We learn from such examples that sounds that are easy to distinguish aurally are not always as easy to distinguish in the visual domain.

The oldest method of species identification is vocal mimicry. After vocal imitation comes imitation by mechanical means. Certain musical instruments trace back to acoustic decoys. The ocarina modelled in the shape of a pigeon produces a soft, cooing noise, and can be used to lure a plump bird into a snare. The duck call is a double-reed mouthpiece related, via the Renaissance shawm, to the cor anglais chosen by Prokofiev to represent the character of Sasha the duck in *Peter and the Wolf*. The horn celebrated in the epic deeds of Roland and Robin Hood, and still in use as a ceremonial instrument in a number of world religions, produces a sound resembling the alarm cry of an ox or deer, evoking the idea of the religious community as a flock. Instruments designed to reproduce the sounds of animals are often fashioned to look like them, on the principle of visual form following acoustic function. Other instruments crafted from animal parts, such as the drum, are imbued with the character of the animal from which the material is taken.

The manufacture of instruments for imitating animals freed language from the cumbersome task of direct imitation and also created a repertoire of acoustic valves, switches, coupling devices, and resonators that in addition to serving as models for developing instruments specifically for musical entertainment, also established a pool of knowledge applicable in science and engineering.

After imitation comes naming. A name is at one or more remove from the object named. It has meaning for the person who gives the name, but not for the species itself. One can communicate with animals by reproducing the sounds they make. Children moo and baa conversationally with cows and sheep. Parrots and budgerigars imitate the voices of their pet human beings. We distinguish pet names from species names. Pet names are individual call-signs. They represent the individual as an acoustic monogram, and from the point of view of the budgerigar, identify the food provider. Species names no longer serve the function of identifying with the animal kingdom as a repertoire of recognizable sounds.

Had Adam in Eden called the first parrot Polly, the first dog Rover, the first cow Daisy, etc., creation might have turned out rather differently. But in the legend he went further than that. Giving proper names to the flora and fauna of creation is an act of asserting the primacy of humankind. The capacity to name names entails, by implication, a right to interpret the world as a place where human distinctions are those that matter. The naming of creation and concomitant making of distinctions is the foundation on which the development of language, and thereafter science and government, are all based. The biblical loss of innocence and consequent fall from grace of humanity are inevitable consequences of a naming process the effect of which is to alienate humankind from the rest of creation. It is not necessary to justify the fall by blaming Eve for betraying Adam after being seduced by the serpent. That gloss on sin is unnecessary, and in any case after the fact. The Tree

of Knowledge is superfluous to the critical act of naming names and
its terrible implications for human self-awareness, and could just as
easily be a diversion invented by a priesthood anxious to distance
itself from the taint of original sin attaching to a practised expertise
in making intellectual distinctions.

Sounds are self-referential, because the human ear is an acoustic
filter distributing the pattern of frequencies comprising a given signal to a corresponding array of frequency-sensitive nerve sensors.
Each sound automatically impresses its unique stamp on a listener's
awareness (though not automatically on conscious memory). The
transition from being conscious of a sound to being aware of its special character relies on introspection: it is after the event, and it is a
judgement applied to the after-effects of the event. The after-effects
of hearing, as of any other sensory impression, are real but internal,
and arise from short-term changes of state in the activity of neural
sensors and relays conveying a sound impression from ear to brain.
With practice in monitoring these after-effects a listener may learn
to make extremely refined distinctions between different sounds
heard simultaneously as well as similar sounds heard successively.

Sounds are also self-referential in respect of the person listening.
Descartes could just as easily have remarked 'I hear, therefore I am',
belonging to a tradition regarding thought as inconceivable without words, and words inconceivable without sound. It is a valid
point. If the act of naming names is an act of self-alienation from
the things named, then merely thinking in terms of names that refer
to the world is sufficient to demonstrate one's conscious independence of the rest of creation, which is what one assumes Descartes
was seeking to establish.

In fact noises will do just as well as names. The difference in precision of vocabulary is simply one of degree. Making noises is part
of the process of self-assertion from infancy to maturity and
beyond. In communicating a view of the world in intelligible
speech, serious-minded individuals continue to pursue an infantile
agenda of self-assertion for which the meaning of language is irrel-
evant. The humour of Ionesco and the tragicomedy of Beckett rely
on a sense of language as paradoxically self-instantiating and self-
isolating. To describe others as being in love with the sound of their

own voice is to say that they are talking primarily in order to reinforce their sense of self, and only incidentally, if at all, to say anything of interest or use. But we all do that, up to a point. There is an art of responding to interview that relies on the assumption of the listener that whatever is asserted is the answer to the question that has been asked. The act of vocalizing, whether speaking in tongues or selling toothpaste, is first an act of self-determination, and only after that a gesture of communication.

Myth and legend emphasize the acoustic richness of creation. The gods declare. The wizard utters an incantation. Things exist and happen because the responsible agency says so. The corollary to believing in creation by decree is that the sounds of creation are proof of the reality of a creator. The scriptural injunction 'let everything that hath breath praise the Lord' can also be construed as a statement of fact. Given that sounds of every kind express the reality of creation, the reciprocal must also be true, that the reality of creation corresponds in the physical domain to reverberations of the voice of the creator that caused them to come into existence.

We can apply the same analogy to human perception of a world of sounds. In our capacity as hearing animals we rely on the evidence of sounds of creation for assurance of our own continuing existence as sane and sentient beings. In hearing we recognize our ability to hear and our relationship with the world at large. Moreover, we rely on hearing sounds to guide our everyday actions, as well as to communicate. Perceived changes in the appearance of sounds, or in our ability to process sounds, are indications of changes in our relationship with the world and our ability to function successfully in the world.

There is a problem. It is that in order for objects to be named, they have to be distinguished, and the process of making distinctions cannot logically entail knowing in advance that the distinctions exist, or having names for them. The problem is twofold. On the procedural side, in order to describe a perception the philosopher has to interrupt the very line of enquiry on which the insight depends. To say 'Eureka!' is to signal a successful conclusion, but to formulate the same conclusion requires a mental break from the process of investigation. Putting a new insight into words for the first time is in effect saying 'this is a perception as I remember doing it a moment ago'. A reflection by definition cannot coexist with the behaviour it reflects upon; furthermore, a verbal formulation of a perception from memory arguably cannot convey the total impact of an insight that at the time of being experienced was non-verbal. There is a double dislocation: one of time, the other of language.

The second problem is where to begin. The world accessible to perception is continuous. People continue to monitor the environment even while they sleep. At any one time what and how an individual perceives may be affected by prior habituation. It simply will not do to represent any perception as an instantaneous event.

At the start [of *Tractatus*] we are told that the world is all that is the case: a totality of facts, not merely a totality of things. The world cannot be identified with a totality of things, since the totality of things can constitute a variety of worlds depending on their arrangement. At this point, however, we cannot say with confidence what Wittgenstein means by saying that 'the world *is* the facts' for we have yet to be told what the facts are. (Fogelin 1976: 3)

I am not altogether persuaded that 'the world being a totality of facts' is what Wittgenstein actually means by 'the world being all that is the case'. There is a difference in perception between being as an entirety and being as a collection of parts, however variously described. Musical perceptions are different in emphasis, if not in nature, from visually orientated perceptions. Wittgenstein came from a musical family (his brother was the celebrated concert pianist Paul Wittgenstein) and his philosophical starting-point alludes to a musical sensibility. He begins with a global perception, just as if one were listening to a performance of music one would start with a global perception of (say) its key. But there is a paradox in Wittgenstein that is also found in a musical context. A listener perceives that a music has harmony or loudness or rhythm without necessarily recognizing that the harmony or loudness or rhythm are identifiable with particular elements, either individually or as a totality. It is plausible in a visual context to say that a still life is a beautiful work of art, and to go on from there to say that its beauty resides in the artist's treatment of particular images within the composition: a bowl, a bottle, a loaf, a piece of fruit, a tablecloth, etc. These are images from everyone's experience. With a musical experience this is not necessarily the case. How many listeners can identify a harmonious effect as a particular type of chord, or a particular combination of instruments? And what would it mean if they were able to do so? It is much less plausible to try to argue that an impression of harmony in music resides in the artist's treatment of a particular combination of pitches and tone qualities. Somehow the argument doesn't carry the same force, because for a majority of listeners harmony is manifest but pitches and tone qualities are not. They hear the global quality, but are unable to relate it to any content.

The curious fascination Wittgenstein holds for an older generation of English philosophers may have to do with the world-view of a more actively musical culture. He understands things differently, and he understands different things from the inhabitants of 'das Land ohne Musik'. To a serious thinker of Wittgenstein's Austrian upbringing, music means a certain kind of perception of the structure of civilized life as inclusive, dynamic, and ultimately harmonious. In defining the world as all that is the case, Wittgenstein may be drawing on the musical aspect of his cultural background in a desire to be totally succinct, transparent, and non-controversial. One can only risk that degree of concentration and transparency in observations that one believes to be self-evident.

A musician may recognize the priorities embedded in Wittgenstein, in particular, a view of the world—the world of our perceptions—as initially unitary. That is not the same as perceiving the world as a totality of facts. A totality of facts, by contrast, is the outcome of a rationalization: a sequential ordering, implicating time (in which to accumulate the totality from the individual facts), and space (to ensure that individual facts are separately accounted for). A knowledge of facts (or even things) is inconsistent with a perception of the world as unitary. We maintain the two ideas—of a unitary world, and of the world as a collection of parts—as a balance of opposing forces; nevertheless the idea of a unitary world is bound to take precedence, since it is on the basis of an underlying unity of the world that identification of component facts or things depends, as a knowledge of the stars depends on a prior acceptance of the idea of the night sky, the firmament, or the heavens.

The only possible definition of 'all that is the case', meaning all that we perceive, at the instant of perception, is the negative 'what I am not'. We are back with the theme of naming as an act of self-alienation. My face in the mirror is not me, neither is the hand I hold in view. These things at that moment belong to the revealed world, however connected to me they are in a physical sense. It follows that anything not perceived at a given instant, even though available to the senses, is not 'the world' but an other-world, corresponding to 'the self'. The self is all that is contained and not expressed. The world, in this sense, is understood as the reciprocal of the self. The world reciprocates. I and the world are reciprocal. The philosopher's world is an expression of self-determination, which is also self-denial. Self-definition is also self-rejection. Happily, self-alienation is not a permanent tribulation, as it was for poor old Adam and Eve, but a continuous, voluntary, and beneficial process the loss of which is destructive (see Sacks 1973, *passim*).

In distinguishing the world as unitary from the world as a collection of facts, one is able to avoid the difficulty of identifying 'all that is the case' with 'a totality of facts (or things)', since the existence of constituent facts or things is not established by the statement that the world is all that is the case. Identification of facts or things depends on a prior assumption of the existence of a world that is the reciprocal of the self. An infant at the crawling stage, no less than a chicken in the farmyard, octopus in a laboratory tank, or goldfish in a bowl, will move towards, seize, and taste an unfamiliar object that appears in its field of vision. Visually directed activity leads to the identification of specific things. Behaviour of this sort is said to acknowledge an outside world by virtue of the object of attention provoking the action; but for the action to be initiated in the first place requires a presupposition, however primitive, of the world. That facts or things comprise a totality, one moreover corresponding to the world, can be inferred without reference to what the things are. The world is not a creature of the facts, therefore, as the facts are of the world.

'The problem of other minds', according to Peter Carruthers, 'consists in an argument purporting to show that we can have no knowledge of any other conscious states besides our own' (Carruthers 1986: 7). In simple terms, 'I cannot know what you are thinking, even though we may agree on what we are talking about, and may even agree in our views on what we are talking about'. Does it matter? Well, yes it does matter, if language and communication is to mean anything, that what we say should be understood for what we intend it to mean. Using language involves an assumption that others can understand what we have in mind through what we say. Understanding what another person has in mind, however, does not necessarily involve a knowledge of what that person is saying, what exactly it refers to in the person's life experience, or whether it makes logical or grammatical sense. All the same, these things may help. Inasmuch as language is a co-operative enterprise, the more someone appears to make sense, the better the co-operative result, but in the long run it is the nature and degree of co-operation achieved that declares most emphatically and with least room for doubt what measure of understanding is attained along the way. Paradoxically, the greater reliability of co-operative action as an index of common understanding rests in large part on the absence of a regulating text.

Asked for whom he composed, Stravinsky replied, 'Myself and the hypothetical other' (Stravinsky and Craft 1959: 91). For the self, composing is a necessary act of expression arising from an urge to realize musical ideas in audible form. As for the hypothetical other, a musical composition is an experience shared: in the interim with an interpreter, and in the long run with an audience. The ideal interpreter is one who understands and has the technical ability to translate a composer's manuscript into sound. Mere reading is not enough, since musical notation is itself an incomplete medium, but in composing with an ideal interpreter in mind a composer is tacitly acknowledging that what information notation is able to convey has a duty to respect the physical limitations of human performers and their instruments, and to present that information as potentially intelligible in itself—which is to say, to make his intentions as clear as possible. A performer by definition is an involved intermediary, through whom notes on paper are realized as actions that in turn influence the production and emission of acoustic images. We are used to the idea of singers assuming the personalities represented in the roles they do well. It seems perfectly natural because a text entails a human situation, and a voice a persona, and both are given coherence and meaning because the language of a text is something an audience does understand. It is not quite so easy to account for interpretations of purely instrumental music. The gestural language of violin playing, for example, cannot identify as directly or intimately with the imagery of human emotion as a voice may do almost by default. In the absence of a text, what is left is a behaviour pattern brought to focus and modified to pass as it were through the lens of an instrument. The absence of a text does not render a musical score necessarily unintelligible or meaningless (though self-expression through music and without language may give rise to behaviour of a kind that in other contexts would run the risk of being interpreted as abnormal, and even autistic). Performance imposes on the performer a duty to elucidate those aspects of a composition that intelligibility entails, such as consistent intonation, repetition and variation, regularities of tempo and phrasing, balance, and symmetry.

In the past, interest has focused on whether music could be shown to resemble language. Perhaps the question to be asked is whether language resembles music, rather than the other way round. Musical intelligibility works according to different rules. The composer is satisfied by certain aspects of musical shape. The literal meaning of a composition is a composer's score. Notation is like a language in that it invokes a repertoire of interpretative conventions, but is unlike a language in that the meanings attaching to musical notation do not inhere in notation, but in performance. That is to say, pitch and time values are not meanings. Live performance adds human dimensions of gesture and timing, both of which entail a sense of narrative continuity as a by-product of the performance taking place within the continuity of experience of the performing artist. For someone reading a novel, the same correspondence of narrative time and reading time does not obtain. In all other respects the basis of musical communication is not a meaning inherent in the score, but a potential for meaning to be realized.

Those whose terms of verification are words and their meanings, and sentence structures and their implications, may not be too happy with the argument that language is an imperfect medium of enquiry, or that what words actually mean is of only secondary importance to the effect they obtain. That language in practice *does* work as though to convey what is in another's mind is, after all, part of the reason why philosophy and psychology devote so much attention to finding out how it does so. That language *ought* to work, equally, is an understandable response to the discovery that, on balance, we cannot know for certain that it does. The moral imperative weather balloon expands and generates more lift the higher we climb and the thinner the atmosphere of rational enquiry. In practice, language works, the criterion being as a medium of communication. On that basis it is considered reasonable to adduce that language and its structures resemble, as well as represent, thoughts and thinking processes, and furthermore, that there is scope for developing language as a precision instrument as a means of improving the precision of thinking.

In identifying 'the problem of other minds' with 'an argument purporting to show that we can have no knowledge of any other conscious states besides our own', a failure of understanding (the problem of mind) is equated with a failure of language (to demonstrate unambiguous knowledge of the conscious states of others). If it were not a failure of language, it would not be a failure of understanding, since whatever else it might be, language would be able to convey it adequately. There are other clues. A definition of thinking as consisting of individually knowable conscious states, is a definition of thinking in language terms, in fact dictionary terms. Digging deeper, we arrive at a structure of language communication as a matching of conscious states. I have a conscious state of what it is we are talking about, you also have a conscious state, and if they match, we understand one another. Or not, as the case may be.

The force of the matching of minds analogy derives from a shared assumption about a real world environment in which both I and you coexist as individuals. But the logical corollary of saying that we can never know any other conscious state besides our own is that we can only know our own conscious state. By definition, that conscious state includes other people.

There are two lines of development leading from such a formulation. The first addresses the degree of otherness of the other people to whom we attribute conscious states that may be different from our own. Their thoughts are manifested in terms of agreement and disagreement, not in relation to our thoughts, which are by definition insufficiently explicit or knowable in themselves, but to the intentions, actions, and consequences predicated by them. Paraphrasing Bergson, we know of the existence of other thoughts by the resistance of others to the realization of our desires (i.e. what our thoughts entail).

The second line of inference drawing on the notion that our knowledge of our own thinking includes the knowledge attributed to others, leads to the view that the existence of other minds and alternative mental states is not, after all, a relevant consideration. In practice, we behave as though other minds do not matter, effectively, as though they don't exist. That on reflection we recognize that other people exist, and have thoughts and motives, and act agreeably and co-operatively, is a separate issue. What matters at the time is achieving a viable concordance of actions to achieve a personal goal. In that regard the thoughts of others are subsumed in our own intentions.

That being the case, the proposition of other conscious states than our own becomes meaningless. The real question is how we have knowledge of other consciousnesses than our own, or more precisely, how we distinguish that part of our consciousness that resists our desires from a remainder subject to conscious direction. That is one way of saying that the external world manifests itself as a reciprocal consciousness. Not a neutral environment, or world of objects, including other people who have thoughts to which we do not have access, but an extension of our own consciousness that happens to declare its other-worldliness by the way it responds to our intentions and actions. The existence of an other-world is predicated by awareness of the self. The world is everything that is 'not-self'. That does not make it an objective reality, since my self-hood (body space) includes the world and may expand or contract in range depending on how I happen to feel, or what task I may be engaged upon.

In being conscious of myself as distinct from a world including other people, so I may be led to conclude that the world is also conscious of itself as distinct from me. Not dead, not empty, but alive and aware: the 'world soul', as Plato expressed it. What is the evidence for a conscious world? This is not a late conversion to the Gaia hypothesis. First, it is logically entailed by subjective experience: the world as I experience it directly is the world of my personal perceptions, and not an objective representation. It follows that any remainder left over from that part of my world that I recognize as my self, is also a living subjectivity. Second, the world apart from my self behaves consistently towards my self, in offering resistance and setting limitations on what my independent self can do, such as leaping a tall building at a single bound, running faster than a speeding bullet, and so on. It is arguably more rational to conclude that the world is conscious than to conceive of it as objectively neutral, since the latter alternative forces on us the idea of an objective world at one further remove from the reciprocal subjective world, an objective world whose existence is permanently unverifiable (which is almost where we came in).

Language allows us to interrogate the world, in particular that part of the reciprocal self that corresponds to other people. That process of interrogation leads to an accumulation of positive and negative responses, and among them, indications of agreement about things as being external to 'other people' in the same way as they are external to the self.

However, the flip side of a world of objects including other people that are both in the consciousness of the self and reciprocal to other events within the consciousness of the self, is the notion of the self and other people as portions of the experience of a higher, 'parental' self-consciousness. That change of perspective enables other people to be regarded as real individuals and not creatures of the imagination. Since other people behave as though they are autonomous beings, the new perspective makes it easier to deal with them. The advantage of so doing is offset, needless to say, by a corresponding loss of sense of personal authority, and the possibility of conflict arising between the self in control, who is ultimately isolated, and the member of the group, who assumes the status of a divine fiction.

That being the case, the argument that we can have no knowledge of any other conscious state besides our own, is met by the counter-arguments (1) that having knowledge of our own conscious state entails knowledge of an external world that manifests consciousness, and (2) the theological point that the self and others are equal manifestations of a superior 'global awareness', from which it is clear that the term 'self-consciousness' is a misnomer.

We therefore distinguish a sense or conviction of the objective reality of the world from an expression of objective knowledge of its existence. The sense of objective reality is continually reinforced by the persistence of observable features in our sensory experience, and the fact that they remain consistent to experience despite errors and imperfections in processing sensory data, and even despite death. So divinity is 'human' by inference and humanity created in the image of the divine by corollary. 'As for the self, so for the world; inasmuch as I know, so am I also known.'

8

Unison

> The most interesting philosophical question [Jacques de Liège] addresses (in *Speculum musicae* I.26) is whether two notes sounded in unison can be called 'different sounds'.
>
> (Burnett 1991: 63)

THE most elementary form of harmony, and also the highest, is the unison. Unison is two or more voices or musical instruments sounding at the same pitch. Its earliest expression is infant mimicry. Its most obvious expression in ordinary life is chanting by rote and group singing. Unison means absence of interval. Among aural cultures the sound of a person or object is proof of its physical existence at a particular place in the immediate vicinity (within hearing) of a listener. Detection of sound is also confirmation of the environment. On television, the sight of a stately ballroom or cathedral is just an image; add sound and reverberation—virtually any sound will do: a voice, a banging door, footsteps, music even—and the image becomes a location with which a viewer can readily identify.

When two or more voices sing in unison they are in effect occupying the same pitch space. For aural cultures, therefore, unison singing is charged with mystery, since it manifests the paradoxical idea that two or more bodies can occupy the same physical space. There is a further complication arising from the fact that voices or instruments of contrasting timbre, despite their differences, are still able to achieve a unison. Since voice and instrument are different in sound as well as in appearance and material structure, the puzzle is how any unison can be recognized, let alone attained.

It can be argued that voices in unison are insubstantial and do not therefore interact, so the paradox that they occupy the same space is an illusion. The most common example of a unison is that of a musical tone and its reverberation in a resonant environment. In principle the reflected sound is not of the same substance as the original sound, just as the face reflected in a mirror is insubstantial compared to the face in real life. However it doesn't work out like that. In practice a steady tone such as a trumpet note does meet and combine with its reflection from an adjacent wall to produce an aural checkerboard pattern of alternating zones of loud and soft where the signals interact either to reinforce one another or cancel one another out. In acoustics, therefore, the reflection is of the same substance as the original, because it is capable of interacting with it.

Albertus [Magnus] puts forward an original question concerning whether sounds hitting each other in the air destroy one another . . . It is a matter of experience that these sounds do *not* corrupt each other, but the reason is difficult to explain. [It cannot be] that sound has a spiritual being, because when it is conveyed in the medium it has to behave according to the nature of the medium, one of whose requisites is that two different figures cannot exist in the same place at the same time. (Burnett 1991: 59)

Unison voices and instruments remain separated and distinct objects in the visible and material world. But Albertus is also considering the interference of 'high' and 'low' sounds, and he concludes that some cancellation may arise, but that enough uncancelled sound leaks round the edges for both to continue to be heard. It is unclear whether by high and low Albertus simply means sounds an octave apart or high and low voices in unison (e.g. the same note as sung by male and female singers). One suspects he means a bit of both. Different harmonics coexist in the same vibrating string or air column, and they can be the same pitch or different pitches in harmonious relationship. If their occupying the same space is an illusion, however, the fact of the unison cannot be explained in terms defending the coincidence of visible and aural worlds. It can only be explained by postulating an alternative reality for acoustic events, a reality in which unison bodies are able to occupy the same space. Even string harmonics, which coexist in the same string, occupy distinct physical locations.

According to the two-worlds hypothesis the audible universe, the invisible reality open to hearing and accessible to music and the human voice, is a higher and separate reality from the physical world of our other perceptions. It is a higher reality because it manifests harmony as a basic condition of being; it is a separate reality because it is seemingly indifferent to many of the usual physical constraints of substance and space. The significance of the unison being achieved between different beings (different voices or instruments) lies in the expression of the idea of beings separated in physical space coming together in unity in acoustic space, the realm of the divine. Since the acoustic realm is invisible but also a region of physical interaction, the corollary of attaining a unison in the acoustic domain is an ideal of physical union with the divine. The next question is how the idea of physical union can be realized. It is clearly a desirable objective, in so far as the idea of a harmonious material world is a desirable goal. It is a human objective, since harmony is a human perception; it is an objective that by definition focuses on the 'flesh', i.e. the physical being and its frailties, in the service of transcending the flesh, i.e. rising above, and attaining a condition of being that is free of, physical desires and constraints. To human beings who are of necessity physical beings the first option is embracing a saintly life-style of self-denial. The implacable logic of an objective of union with the divine leads inevitably, however, to the ultimate self-denial, which is death, represented for many by a particular death by crucifixion, and associated doctrine of personal salvation. The crucifixion in these terms is a logical as well as a theological necessity, and is symmetrical with the idea of absolute personal goodness. The doctrine of the resurrection is thus not a fanciful addition to a human tragedy, but a necessary consequence of the same logical position.

The story of the crucifixion turns on the relationship between acoustic and physical worlds, and on the human difficulty of effecting a reconciliation between the two. In the mechanical world of musical acoustics, unison and harmony relationships express stable states. Harmonics on a string are always at the same fixed locations. If the quill point finds such a location, the harmonic spontaneously appears, as though switched on. Move the point away from that location, no matter how slightly, and the harmonic vanishes, and all you feel is a vibrating string. Achieving a unison is a voluntary act: you have to intend it, and you have to learn to achieve it. Achieving a unison is making the transition from a state of awareness of oneself as a separate individual to a sense of disembodied identity with the sound which, being of the same pitch, both reinforces the voice and gives the impression of locating the unison in a region outside the body (in the way that a stereo image appears to occupy the space between the two speakers). Out-of-body experiences of such a kind suggest that the transition from a condition of selfhood to a condition of union with the divine can be effected painlessly and instantaneously, either voluntarily (e.g. by confession), or through a ritual of touching and tuning the individual to the divine will. What is interesting to reflect on is the apparent ease of transition to union with the divine associated with the rites of religion, in contrast to the extreme physical discomfort, abuse, and eventual death suffered by the victim of crucifixion. It is surely not enough to gloss over the discrepancy in suffering by saying that one person's suffering is able to do duty for anybody else's to an extent that nobody else is required to undergo any suffering at all. Suffering by proxy can hardly be defended as an example to follow, if in practice it serves as a licence to avoid suffering in the first place, which is morally questionable. 'The assiduous practice of self-mastery and the most sparing indulgence in the pleasures of sense are the "philosophic life" which the Greek spirit recommends as the highest. The best Greeks would blame the life of an English clergyman, professor, or philosopher as too self-indulgent' (Dean Inge, in Livingstone 1921: 47). But our concern is not the moral issue, rather the integrity of the unison analogy. In order for the human suffering of the crucifixion to be justified doctrinally, we have to have stronger evidence of an intervening state, on the way to achieving unison, that can be shown to correspond to a condition of physical suffering.

Such a state is familiar to singer-instrumentalists, guitar vocalists, and folk harpists, who sing to their own accompaniment and are used to monitoring the unison of voice and instrument from close quarters. It is also familiar to piano-tuners, who work with sets of multiple strings tuned to the same pitch, and to brass players from experience of tuning their individual instruments to a common reference tone. In the realm of traditional music-making, there is no easy route to perfect tuning. Audiences take for granted the harmonious sound of an orchestra or the rich, full consistency of tone of a piano, but that harmony and richness depend on prior tuning. Tuning is a painstaking affair involving much sampling and cautious manœuvring in regions of dissonance and potential aural distress on either side of true pitch.

The aim of good tuning is the same: achieving a blending of tone and identity of pitch between voices and instruments that denotes a supervening identity and harmony of purpose. In musical practice, however, especially among young learners, deviations from good tuning inevitably occur, and they do have a painful effect on the listener. It is a non-physical pain, but none the less real. An out-of-tune note on a piano, or two trumpets sounding a microtone apart, can also be unpleasant to hear. Interference effects would certainly have been familiar to classical philosophers, whose experiments in acoustics were conducted on a wide range of instruments ancestral to those of the modern orchestra. Out of this background of specialized and general musical experience, therefore, arises the knowledge and acceptance of a danger zone standing in the path of all those musical pilgrims attempting to come together in unison. We should not therefore be surprised at the idea of the passage to self-enlightenment involving a transitional period of trial and suffering.

The reality of interference of tones deviating from perfect unison would seem to entail an equivalent danger zone or transitional state separating the physical realm of individual voices from the sanctified condition of disembodied unison, a zone moreover of physical suffering, by analogy with the physical interference of discordant tones. The characteristic throbbing and harshness of tone associated with deviation from the unison is the physical manifestation of the trial to be endured in order for unison to be successfully achieved. That transition is preserved in the musical convention of the trill on the leading note, leading to resolution in the tonic. It is represented symbolically in the bible story of Jacob wrestling with the angel, and his associated vision of a stairway connecting earth and heaven, the physical world and the aural world, a recognizable image of a musical scale by which humanity gains entry to communion with the divine. Jacob's vision of the ladder or stairway, also the subject of a visionary cantata by Schoenberg, incorporates angels ascending and descending, signifying a scale of which every degree or note is sanctified as a harmonic.

In human terms, being on the edge of making the unison is more significant than achieving the unison. This is a purely practical observation, though its theological implications are also curiously interesting. The art of melodic expression in musical cultures across the world is based on techniques of deliberate bending and distortion of the unison or harmonious interval. Communication also involves distorting the unison, because distorting the unison is necessary for self-expression as well as for self-consciousness. A voice that diverges from unison is asserting its individuality and claiming for itself a substantial existence and distinct location in space. A voice that falters out of tune is also revealing its humanity. Being mortal, we are subject to mortal emotions.

Bagpipes, paired trumpets, Gregorian chant, and modern telecommunications all convey information as a modulation of a carrier frequency. Information is conveyed in monotone plainchant as variation in timbre associated with the changing vowels of a text. Vowel changes in a text are more or less random: there is a trade-off between musical and textual intelligibility. A folk instrument such as a jew's harp allows the timbres of different vowel sounds to be organized into acceptable melodies without the constraining influence of a text. Music for bagpipes superimposes a variable melody or chant on to a fixed drone. At signalling distances the combination is perceived as a constant tone subject to vowel-like modulation. These instruments correspond to communications devices; they do not associate, other than symbolically, with the expression of emotion. The melodic inflections of Gregorian chant play a formal and grammatical, rather than an expressive role. In radio and telecommunications similar procedures and associations prevail. The listener tunes in to a channel by matching a receiver's choice of frequency to the frequency of transmission. That frequency is modulated to convey intelligible speech and music. Distortions in reception arising from interference with an adjacent channel are perceived as a loss of information and a characteristic wave-like surging in and out of resolution. There are other similarities. The world of broadcasting is perceived as omnipresent and, to a greater or lesser degree, as an overseeing intelligence. Audiences develop a sense of close personal relationship with media personalities, and identify firmly with the environments of favourite programmes.

As well as allowing for the transmission of intelligence, acoustic signals that manœuvre around the unison tend to communicate more effectively at a distance than unmodulated signals, or signals that maintain a consistent unison. The characteristically approximate unison between a pair of Tibetan long trumpets is not due to primitive workmanship or lack of musicianship, as ears attuned to Western priorities of tuning might initially suppose. The gongs of Balinese music are designed to exploit amplitude modulation, either in the complex vibration patterns of individual instruments, or between pairs of instruments that differ slightly in tuning (Schneider and Beurmann 1993: 202). These instruments and techniques expressing signalling functions in mountainous and forested regions are bound to evolve in ways appropriate to the open air and transmission distances of a rural environment, just as orchestral instruments and techniques of Western music have adapted to the enclosed spaces and lesser distances of concert halls. A fluctuating signal generated by a pair of long trumpets in approximate unison can be more readily detected at a great distance than the same instruments in exact unison, where no inharmonicity is produced. Exact unison, as in the case of the sound from distributed multiple speakers in an open-air public-address system, produces zones of mutual reinforcement and cancellation in the surrounding area, which is why you can hear announcements clearly in certain places but not in others. Deviation from absolute accuracy, like high-end 'dither' in CD recordings, or vibrato in performing style, reduces the unwanted effects of unison between separated channels, and can also allow for meaningful fluctuations of tone to be produced in a controlled manner by microtonal variations in pitch rather than by changes in power. The inharmonicity of steeple bells serves a similar purpose. In addition to extending audible range, it represents a more efficient use of available energy. It is why pianos are tuned out of unison to make the tone more interesting, more penetrating, and longer-lasting. The hammer striking three or four strings tuned to a controlled approximation of the same pitch initiates a complex vibration that feeds on itself and evolves in an acoustically interesting fashion, creating a sense of pleasing liveliness of tone and full reverberation. When multiple strings are tuned precisely in unison, which is normal for the harpsichord and 18th-century fortepiano, the result is a focused, precise tone, thinner in quality, of immediate response and rapid decay without audible residue—a sound more suited, in consequence, to smaller concert chambers and to a contained, classical aesthetic.

As two electronic signals gradually diverge in pitch from an initial unison, the tone begins to wow, that is, slowly fluctuate in amplitude. As the two signals continue to draw apart, the wow accelerates to a flutter, then to a buzz, thereafter separating into distinct pitches with the buzz becoming audible as a gradually rising difference tone in the bass. Combination and summation tones are also produced when two tones are in perfect harmony, though not in unison. The tones of two trumpets or natural horns sounding a perfect fifth apart produce a combination tone an octave lower than the lower tone; the top two notes of a major triad generate the missing key note, again an octave lower. In some instances the combination tone is pitched between the two. Traditional fanfares using natural (non-valve) trumpets are designed to produce combination tones in the ears of those listening, often to stirring effect. The implication of combination tones being produced as a consequence of achieving a relationship of perfect harmony is a mythology of physical union (because the two pitches remain distinctively different in pitch) sanctified by the presence of a third tone in harmony with both. This is not a marriage and birth analogy. Rather, it conveys the idea of individuals in relationship, and a sense of that intervallic relationship as a physical and audible presence between them. In Schubert's *Eine kleine Trauermusik*, for instance, the combination tone produced by two natural horns symbolizes the absent friend whose death is being mourned.

Self-evidently, acoustic space is commensurate with physical space up to the point where unison is achieved. The transition from close interval to interference to unison can be understood as an acoustic trial by fire through which the individual must pass to find a sublimated identity on a higher plane. The symbolism of the unison has to do therefore with transcending a material reality in order to attain a state of grace. Belief in the transcendence of material reality entails a prior acceptance of the idea that sounds correspond to substantial entities. Symmetry requires that corresponding mysteries obtain in the physical domain. Human bodies are subject to possession by disease and malign spirits. They are spirits because they occupy the same physical space as the person afflicted, and are malign because they cause patterns of interference as a consequence of the physical disharmony they inflict on the bodily 'soundness' of the patient. Trembling, groaning, repetitive actions, periodic crises all correspond, to an aurally aware culture, to effects of acoustic interference, effects extending to very low-frequency oscillations of a kind that can arouse actual nausea in listeners.

Needless to say, the effects of such 'possession' may also be benign. Sex and the consumption of food are instances of communion in practical life where separate physical beings come together partly or wholly to occupy the same physical space. The interference effects of such union are on the whole pleasurable, leading to the waving gait of those who drink, and in the case of sex, to a different kind of low-frequency oscillation that may lead in due time to the generation of a combination tone in flesh and blood.

It is perhaps not surprising that many social and religious sacraments and taboos relate to possession and food. The fall of Adam, despite the naming of names, is attributed to his eating of the tree of knowledge, a wilful act of assimilating knowledge by physically becoming one with the fruit of the tree. Adam desired divine knowledge, only to learn that attaining divinity entailed human suffering. Eating entails suffering. And not only eating, but sex as well: according to doctrine any form of bodily union is sacramental and congruent with mortification of the flesh. The acoustic analogy is plain. The complementary act is celebration of the eucharist. The ritual consumption of wafer and wine expresses an identity of being with one whose human suffering mandates believers to aspire to union with the creator. As a sacrament translating from the acoustic into the material domain, the eucharist has a force of conviction similar to the myths of the creation and incarnation. It stands for a conversion of perception of the material world in relation to the invisible (acoustic) world. Instead of treating the material or substantial world as the enduring reality of which sounds are no more than a passing reverberation, the communicant is encouraged to regard the invisible domain of word and sound as the ultimate reality, of which material existence is a transitory echo. The inversion of normal perceptions is stated time and again in the scriptures. Material existence, worldly goods, and the pleasures of the flesh, contrary to appearances, are vanities that pass; the domain of the (spoken) Word, contrary to human perceptions, is in fact the transcendent reality that calls humanity and all creation into being. This simple inversion has long since been lost to clerical minds for whom the invisible world no longer has the focus in acoustical experience of earlier, preliterate ages. The resulting confusion is partly verbal:

Sometimes the mystic union is taken to be a form of ontological merging; sometimes it is seen as merely as ecstatic experience of union; and sometimes it is interpreted as a close personal relationship in which the individual identity of the partners is preserved and left intact. It is not always easy for interpreters to determine the exact point of these metaphors. (Brümmer 1993: 67)

—and partly intellectual, in that only the material terms are addressed:

The body of Christ becomes present by the substance of the bread's being converted into it (Aquinas used 'conversion' (*conversio*) and cognate words about the Eucharist, not 'change' (*mutatio*).) Aquinas extends the principle [of *materia prima*] to *substantial* change, where we end with a different kind of thing from that with which we began: here too there must be a subject common to the two extremes. This common subject, this matter, is *prime matter*, and the nature of substantial changes shews that prime matter must be *purely potential*. (Fitzpatrick 1993: 9–11)

What Aquinas is wrestling with is the paradox of a material conversion ('prime matter') of a manifestly acoustic conception ('purely potential'), because the reality evidenced in acoustic perceptions is manifestly a reality in potential. However, in the long run the argument just doesn't work in purely material terms.

We have to ask seriously whether rites and beliefs of religion such as creation, incarnation, and transubstantiation were originally so difficult to understand, or whether they have merely been cultivated as mysteries by a medieval clerisy who have lost touch with their acoustic heritage. Is it not possible that the essential mystery of the eucharist is capable of being expressed in simpler and more familiar terms? Is there not a connection between the religious rite and the language of advertising? What is understood by the words: 'Eat this, it will make you better', or 'Drink this, it will make you well?' What is being said here? Other than that in some mysterious way the goodness that is in the food and drink will be taken up and influence the life of the person who eats and drinks. That is surely a sufficient meaning, and it is certainly the kind of meaning that is implied by the correspondence of acoustic and material realities. Arguments from substance are missing the point that the substance is the discarded portion, or waste product: what is retained is the immaterial goodness. The bread is broken to give access to the goodness within. And if goodness is capable of being expressed both in the nature and actions of a human being, and in food that (significantly for the present case) is not raw, and not animal, but processed food from which the outer husk has been removed to leave the germ or essence, transformed beyond visual recognition of its origin (wheat ground and transformed into bread, grapes trodden and strained into wine)—then the miracle of transubstantiation is not a metaphysical conversion of the human being into bread and wine, but an expression of the unison, as it were, of the two kinds of goodness, as between the tones of a human voice and of a manufactured musical instrument. It is the intellectual argument for congruence of acoustic and physical realities that makes a belief in transubstantiation essential. As the physical act of eating (merging bodies) corresponds to the acoustical achievement of unison, so assimilating the material body of Christ is necessarily symmetrical with the idea of achieving unity with his word.

9

Number

ARISTOTLE represented the Pythagoreans as believing that 'all things are number'. What the proposition 'all things (the world) are number (numbers)' is capable of meaning depends on what the Pythagoreans themselves may have meant by 'the world' and 'number'. The universe, or the world, meaning the totality of creation, can mean everything knowable in human terms, or it embraces both the humanly knowable and the humanly imaginable, by sense and by intellect. The meaning of 'number' is another matter altogether. Number in the singular is a term of relationship; numbers in the plural is merely a term for quantities. One is pure mathematics, the other merely accounting.

Arithmetike with the Greeks was distinguished from *logistike*, the science of calculation. . . . *Arithmetike* dealt with numbers in the abstract, and *logistike* with numbered things or concrete numbers . . . [such as] problems about numbers of apples, bowls, or objects generally. (T. L. Heath, 'Mathematics and astronomy', in Livingstone 1921: 107)

Aristotle's view of the Pythagoreans, for whom number is identified with pitch relationships, is to some extent compromised by his own attitude to acoustical events:

Aristotle classifies acts of perceiving, including hearing, as activities complete at any moment, in which respect they are to be distinguished from movements. [He] uses the term *kinesis* rather than *metabole* in his account of hearing. He elsewhere defines *kinesis* as 'the actuality (*entelechia*) of what potentially (*dynamei*) is, as such', a definition which seems designed to capture the distinctive feature of a process that is ongoing, rather than the end-result of that process. (Alan Towey, in Burnett *et al.* 1991: 10)

This is contrary to the Pythagorean equation of numerical with musical, notably pitch relationships. Pitch is frequency, and it is also expressible as length and tension in respect of the monochord. To say of a note played on the harp that it has pitch, is more than just saying it is a sound. To the Pythagorean mind pitch expresses a relationship between length and tension. It also signifies movement, because frequency is understood to be continuous cyclical motion. The Greek model of cyclical motion was the pendulum or the slingshot, a weight swinging or an aerofoil whirring around on a string. The higher the frequency, the faster the speed of rotation. Pitch is thus an expression of speed as well. So number is a term with a world of implication, covering things that are separate and quantifiable, as well as relations between things that cannot be quantified in isolation. We can use this understanding to tease out the meaning of an obscure passage in Philolaus:

Like things and related things did not in addition require any harmony, but things that are unlike and not even related nor of [? the same speed], it is necessary that such things be bonded together by harmony, if they are going to be held in an order. (Huffman 1993: 124)

—which being translated, means that

Unisons and harmonic intervals require nothing added to be harmonious, but intervals that are neither unison nor harmonic (not being related to a common frequency) have to be brought together in harmony, if they are to persist (continue sounding together) in an ordered relationship.

The sense of the passage derives from musical acoustics, in particular observation of the mutual influence and support of the two components of a harmonious interval; but in addition its conclusion extends the analogy of musical acoustics to the harmonious relationship of cycles in nature. Philolaus is arguing that the only way multiple cycles can coexist indefinitely in nature is for them to be in harmony; so it is necessary for the tides, the seasons, and the motions of the planets to conform to an overriding harmony in order for a stable universe to continue to exist. Thus the statement that all things are number declares that the universe is governed by laws of motion that are subject to the laws of harmony.

A universe in perpetual motion is a hard concept to grasp if like Plato and Aristotle you believe in the universe as an orderly, static structure. Perpetual motion begs the question that if the different cycles of the universe co-operate to sustain their harmonious motion, how did that motion start in the first place? The simple answer is that the motion always existed, having no beginning and no end.

Based on Aristotle's evidence we might well have expected that Philolaus' book would have begun with the assertion that 'the cosmos and every-thing in it was constructed out of numbers'. Instead, [it] actually begins 'Nature in the world-order was fitted together out of limiters and unlim-iteds, both the world-order as a whole and everything in it'. (Huffman 1993: 58)

What is meant by 'limiters and unlimiteds'? The plain answer is that they mean quantifiables and non-quantifiables, things that can be numbered and those that are not. The latter include the air and the sea, clouds and light, that are of indeterminate or pervasive extent. One is reminded of Wittgenstein's dictum: 'The world is every-thing that is the case', except that a description of the world com-prised of limiters and unlimiteds seems, if anything, rather more profound.

Quantifiables and non-quantifiables in a visual representation are as images and white space in advertising, that is, as figures and back-ground. But that is somewhat to trivialize the non-quantifiables at the expense of the quantifiables, given the fact that in older civi-lizations, it is the non-quantifiable or unbounded elements of nature that tend to be accorded divine status. As a Pythagorean, Philolaus is attempting more than a static description; Nature is comprehended as a dynamic creation, and an account of Nature would not be complete if it did not make allowance for the move-ment and counter-movement of interrelated periodicities. The acoustic implications take account of the dynamics of natural processes. In musical acoustics, frequency is a measure, and the ratios of harmonics are also quantifiable constants. We also distin-guish human from acoustic measure. Sounds in nature are limited in duration. Duration in sound is an expression of growth and decay, of entropy and the limits of hearing. Frequency is an expression of a transcendental time-scale. Frequency is independent of duration, and yet it is a measure of time. Likewise the tones of a musical instrument, whether a flute or a harp, remain in potential after they have died away, as permanent acoustic features intermittently revealed.

The Greek vision of the universe as a structure of concentric, and in some accounts crystal, spheres is similarly a statement of a transcendent rather than of a literal truth. These people were not deluded visionaries. It is not a way of saying that the stars and planets are attached in reality to rotating glass domes. We have to understand the image as an expression in visual terms of a concept in musical acoustics that the ordinary citizen would have difficulty in grasping, not least because it deals in invisibles. It represents a projection in three dimensions of the paths that would be traced by the harmonic loci or nodes of a musically vibrating stretched string, which is movement essentially in two dimensions. The harmonic points on a stretched string correspond to locations between extremes that in acoustic terms represent zero and infinity, alpha and omega. The Greek universe is a structure of concentric spheres because a sphere is a circular orbit in its totality of possibilities, and the spheres are depicted as crystalline, which is a way of saying that they are transparent to both sight and motion just as the nodes, the defining locations of harmonics on a stretched string, are themselves stable points of reference as well as being transparent to other frequencies.

How real might the metaphor be in acoustic terms? Do crystal spheres vibrate? If so, they would have to flex like a soap bubble and would certainly shatter. Sound propagates as pressure fronts, and pressure fronts need room to expand, and there is no room to expand in a sealed enclosure such as a crystal sphere. A light-bulb about to fail emits a high-pitched musical tone, the sound of an electrical arc oscillating across a break in the filament. The resulting fluctuations in temperature are radiated as pressure fronts that in addition to being transmitted as a high-frequency tone also heat up the air within and may cause the glass to explode. Helmholtz may have had crystal spheres at the back of his mind when he had a glassmaker make him a series of spherical resonators with which to conduct experiments in the analysis and synthesis of complex tones. But in order to function as resonators each Helmholtz sphere has an opening, and the pure tone associated with the spherical shape has to do with the volume of air enclosed rather than with the material of which it is made.

Evidence of serious enquiry into the acoustic properties of crystal spheres can be found in the aptly named *armonica* perfected by Benjamin Franklin. This is a musical instrument consisting of a nesting array of crystal glass hemispheres of graduated size fixed to a spindle and rotated in a trough of water. The instrument is played by friction of the fingertips against the rim of the glasses (according to Greek legend the planetary music of the spheres was also created by friction) producing tones of great purity and intensity on the same principle as playing a wineglass. Gluck, Mozart, Beethoven, and Donizetti composed pieces for it. The instrument's ethereal tones allow a very adequate case to be made for the music of the spheres as an image of an acoustic reality, its pure sounds like harmonics indeed foreshadowing the elemental waveforms of some of the earliest electroacoustic synthesizers of the twentieth century, such as the Telharmonium of Thaddeus Cahill.

But all this is nevertheless beside the point. The crystal spheres were not, and are not, to be taken literally. The Greeks did not experiment with Paris goblets. That succeeding generations of scholars came to interpret the image as a mythical construction of the universe as nesting crystal spheres in audible vibration is simply what happens when literal minds take charge. The new intellectuals like Matthias Herbenus who proclaimed 'the universe gives forth no note', were using a visual irony to debunk traditional aural conventions with which they were no longer comfortable. They refused the image of the crystal spheres not because they could prove it was not true, but because they believed it was not true, and they believed it not to be true because they could no longer conceive how it might ever have been true in any sense. So Herbenus is not being clever or honest in taking the old image literally, but using literalism as a means of distancing himself from that tradition, just as Richard Dawkins in present times seeks to debunk religious myth by taking it literally. It was never essential that the image of the universe be interpreted as a system of solid resonators in audible vibration for it to make sense as an account of the way the planets and stars maintained their courses in the heavens.

On a human, microcosmic scale, the determining influence of number (as distinct from things simply being countable and measurable) is ratio. Ratio is a quantifiable relationship observable between coexistent vibrations, even when their individual frequencies cannot be determined. The Greeks could not measure frequency, but they could determine frequency relationships with considerable accuracy. In the macrocosmic domain, however, the position was reversed: while the periodicities attributable to the tides and seasons and the movements of planets in the cosmos could be measured and predicted to an accuracy of days and fractions of days, it was the relationship of these various macrocosmic periodicities that they were unable to determine for certain, and had to assume to be harmonious. At least they may have appreciated that the 'ultimate cause' or fundamental frequency that would account for the harmonization of the range of observable periodicities in the universe at large would have to be infinitely great, both in energy and in time-scale. The only difference between what the Greeks thought then and what we think now is that today we are making progress toward assigning numerical values both to the Big Bang and to the fundamental frequency (time-span from Big Bang to Big Crunch) of the universe.

To an Aristotelian, the statement 'all things are number' may be taken to mean that all things are quantifiable. But that would be unfair to a Pythagorean like Philolaus, whose knowledge of acoustics and geometry would certainly extend to a variety of non-quantifiable terms ranging from that which is unbounded, like the air; via the practically uncomputable, like grains of sand in the desert; or irrational terms, like π, or the square root of 2 on the hypotenuse of a right-angle triangle of equal sides;—to those terms that remain unknowable because standard measures for them are not in place, of which the most obvious are audible tones whose frequency can be ascertained but not directly quantified, for lack of a measure accurate to fractions of a second. To comment as

Huffman does, that number is of epistemological significance to Pythagoreans, meaning that things 'cannot be known unless through number', is I think an exaggeration. The position represented by what Philolaus actually says, given the complexities of knowledge the Pythagoreans actually possessed, is of a universe of interacting influences of both quantifiables and non-quantifiables, and it carries the Pythagorean implication that the consequence of interaction is a structure of harmonious relationships. That view is certainly familiar to a Renaissance scholar like Kepler, commenting

Numbers are metaphysically and epistemologically inferior to geometrical figures and proportions. Numbers do not exist in physical things, but only 'dispersed units' so exist; numbers are thus abstract, in the sense that an Aristotelian *tabula rasa* mind could develop them by abstraction from the repetitive sense-experience of any kind of unit—they are 'of second, even of third or fourth intention'. (Walker 1978: 43)

A vibrating string has pitch. Pitch we can hear. A modern listener can assign a number to pitch, for example the number 440 to the pitch A above middle C. The number 440 corresponds to the number of vibrations of the string over its entire length in one second. The Pythagorean does not possess a stop-watch and so cannot assign a precise value to frequency. So pitch is real but non-quantifiable.

The vibrating string has length. But length in a string is not a constant in relation to pitch: it can be increased or decreased, the tension varying correspondingly, and still sound at the same pitch. So pitch is also not quantifiable in terms of length. The strings of a violin are all of the same length, but of different pitch, and two adjacent strings can sound at the same pitch by being stopped by the finger at different lengths. (The Pythagoreans were probably the first to ask the question 'how long is a piece of string'.) So length is quantifiable but not commensurate with pitch, even though the pitch of any given vibrating string is partly dependent on its length.

Pitch in a stretched string is also a function of tension. Tension is quantifiable. The weight or force holding a string in tension determines its pitch. Change the force, and you change the pitch of the string. The image of tuning and tension is a metaphor for steadfastness of spirit. 'May the force go with you'. But pitch in itself is no indicator of tension.

Far from consisting of things that can only be known through number, the Pythagorean world consists to a great extent of things that in themselves are unquantifiables, but that when expressed in series or scales of relationships, become quantifiable as *degrees of change*. When the length of a string is varied, by the finger moving up the fingerboard of a guitar or the bridge being moved under the string of a monochord, the change of pitch is in direct proportion to the change in length. When the pitch is changed by altering the tuning of a string, by turning the tuning peg of a violin or guitar,

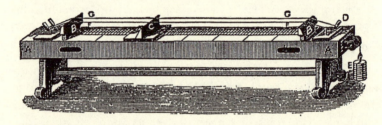

Fig. 1.   A nineteenth-century sonometer or double monochord, one string being tensioned by a tuning peg D, the other string by weights E. From Edmund Catchpool, *Textbook of Sound*, 4th edn. (London, 1903).

or by adding to the weight holding a monochord string in tension, the change in wavelength is inversely proportional to the square root of the change of string tension (Jeans 1937: 64). In saying that the universe of things can only be known in terms of degrees of change, the school of Pythagoras is saying in effect that the universe is only real in so far as it is subject to change. A dynamic universe is a universe in motion. The static universe of conventional wisdom is by the same token unknowable. This is very up-to-date thinking.

Isaac Newton also believed that there was more to Pythagoras and the music of the spheres than fanciful imagery. From accounts of Macrobius and Pliny, he concluded that Pythagoras' proof of harmonic ratios by experiments with weights was an authentic anticipation of his own inverse square law of gravitational attraction. The doctrine of the harmony of the spheres was therefore to be understood as a way of saying that the law governing the motion of the planets was the harmony of weights rather than the harmony of lengths (Walker 1978: 26).

The flight of the arrow and the vibration of the bowstring represent different kinds of motion. In addition to harmonizing the relationship of rotational and linear forces, the Greeks faced the challenge of explaining how the one force might be converted into the other. They deliberated long and hard over whether motion in a straight line and motion in a circle could even be compared. In Aristotle's day, comments Simplicius, it was still a matter of contention whether it was possible for a straight line to be equal to a curve, but the problem was thought to be insoluble and was no longer being seriously discussed. Hence the following:

One might pose the puzzle whether every motion is [comparable with every other or not]. {If indeed they are all comparable, and things moving an equal amount in an equal time are of the same speed, there will be some curved line equal to a straight one, and greater and smaller. Further, an alteration and a locomotion will be equal when in an equal time one thing has been altered and another has been moved locally. Therefore, an affection will be equal to a length, but that is impossible. Is it, then, that things are equal in speed whenever they have moved an equal amount in an equal time, but an affection is not equal to a length, so that an alteration is not equal to a locomotion, nor smaller,} so that not every [motion is] comparable? (Simplicius 1994: 60–1)

To a reader of a modern translation that is not altogether certain of the author's agenda, the topic appears esoteric and its language obscure. Let us imagine it as a slings and arrows question. The motion powering a slingshot is circular motion, whereas (superficially at least) the motion powering an arrow is motion in a straight line (the bowstring). The question is whether the two are directly comparable. Since the whirring sound of a slingshot is different from the twang of a bowstring, the two are not acoustically comparable in cause, though they may be comparable in effect, i.e. the force of the blow, the distance travelled, etc. A sling is held in tension by centrifugal force from a single fixed point, a tension that varies with the speed of rotation and strength of the athlete, and its pitch is thus not a constant. A bowstring by contrast is maintained in tension by the bow between two fixed points, and at every stage from rest to release the string can be heard to produce a tone of determined pitch, that with the aid of a monochord can be assigned a value.

Aristotle may also be comparing the motion of a projectile such as an arrow with the motion that propels it, that of the bowstring, in accordance with the proposition that 'an alteration and a loco-motion will be equal when in an equal time one thing has been altered and another has been moved locally'. This is part of the general question of how force is transferred in nature and of where the forces of nature originally come from. But for Aristotle to cou-ple that with the statement that 'an affection is [not] equal to a length', is apparently to make a direct connection between the ten-sion of the string driving the arrow, and the pitch of the tone pro-duced by the string (as determined by the monochord). The statement is true in so far as the pitch of the string is not directly related to its length, but to a relationship of length and tension. Since the pitch of a monochord string can be altered either by increasing the tension, or by moving the bridge to alter its length, it is true to say that pitch is not equal to length, which interprets the term 'affection' as 'pitch' (in the sense of temperament or intrinsic tension). Aristotle may also be using the term 'affection' as verbal shorthand to make the connection between the pitch of the bowstring and the character of the marksman. One has the distinct impression that a number of concepts are jostling for attention.

In nature, straight-line motion is a characteristic of movement for change, actions that alter the balance of creation and assert the power of one authority over another. The flight of an arrow, the fall of a meteor, the current of a river, the charge of a bull all express the idea of unilateral action in a straight line. Motion in a circle, on the contrary, is associated with stability and control: the spinning top, the slingshot prior to the missile being released, the motion of the planets, etc. In Aristotle, straight-line motion is referred to as alteration, and circular motion as locomotion (motion about a point). By extension, straight-line motion, being associated with the imposition of change, is regarded as dangerous, as the comet is a portent of instability, whereas circular motion, extending to observable cycles in nature involving the sun, moon, the tides, and the seasons, is evidence of stability in the world-order and thus beneficial in effect. Circular motion is motion that is held in place, as a sling holds a shot in rotation; heavenly bodies whose movements are cyclical are *ipso facto* held in place by a connecting power in the centre. We therefore distinguish invasion, which is action for change, from revolution, which is action to restore a primeval stable state. Clearly one way of justifying making war on a neighbouring state would be to represent the action as revolutionary or its instigator as having divine authority. So it is possible to read the story of David and Goliath as the triumph of intelligence over brute force, as expressing the natural superiority of rotational motion (the slingshot) over motion directed in a straight line (spear or sword). David's prowess as a warrior is thus an expression of his skill as a musician.

The dangers of straight-line motion have partly to do with the damage they inflict on the balance of nature, and partly with the loss of direct control once the action is initiated. Force builds to a point of explosive release, the missile is let go, and the marksman then waits to see how far it goes and how well it flies in consequence. In athletics, we distinguish field events, such as the discus, javelin, and hammer, where effort is concentrated in a single action and the missile moves in a straight line as a passive projectile, from track events in which athletes move in orbital motion and rely on powers of speed and endurance consequent on the harmonious interaction of the various parts of the body. Even today, track athletes are more highly paid than field athletes, reflecting a value system that continues to favour the life-style implications of endurance running over those of body-building.

10

Organization

HARMONY is about multiplexing. Multiplexing is information management. For Edison, it was sending more than one telegraph message down a wire at the same time. In music, it is combining several lines of information in such a way that they can be followed independently. Music recognizes a variety of forms of multiplexing, the most basic being voices or instruments in unison, and extending via heterophony (playing the same tune but with individual decoration) through polyphony (playing the same music, but different parts) to counterpoint (multiple parts in call and answer mode based on a melodic model). For harmony to exist there has to be more than one message in transmission. The art of harmony lies in encoding multiple messages so that they do not interfere with one another in transmission and may be successfully decoded as separate strands by whoever is at the receiving end.

In conventional music theory, harmony is vertical thinking: the spacing and combination of notes in a multi-part composition at any given instant. The art of harmonization nevertheless implies a horizontal dimension, the management of multiple layers of information over an extended period, and the rules of harmony are designed to ensure that a balance is maintained between separation of individual lines and harmonic consistency within the group. Among the Greeks harmony in music was the term applied to the rules governing the mode or scale of pitches to which a musical instrument is tuned, rather than rules determining the choice of chord sequences in relation to a melody. By extension, the Greeks regarded harmony in other forms of collective behaviour as an imposed hierarchy within which freedom of action and expression could be sanctioned. Greek harmony thus signified a structure of

standards of behaviour that determined individual scope for interaction rather than rules on how individuals should interact from
moment to moment. Tonality, as the dominating system of early
modern Western music, is our equivalent to harmony in the Greek
sense; what students of music today learn as rules of harmony has
much more to do with regulating a flow of information in multiple parts, and only residually with society or private morals (as in
'modern music is immoral').

Harmony in music is therefore a means of enquiry into the
organization of complex natural phenomena. A sense of harmony
can arise from what appears to be spontaneous obedience to natural
impulse or law (for example, the behaviour of a flock of birds or
shoal of fish moving as a group and avoiding collisions), or alternatively from collective conformity to a signalling authority (soldiers
marching in step, an orchestra under a conductor, etc.). Sheep or
cattle respond collectively to human direction on the road (often
with the aid of musical signals), and revert to individual behaviour
once they are safely arrived in pasture. The purpose of shepherd-
ing a crowd on the road is to keep them moving at the same pace
and toward the same goal. That is what classical harmony implies:
continuity and coherence of collective movement toward a common goal. Having reached the safe haven, however, individual self-
determination becomes the norm. When the limits to freedom are
clearly defined, individuality can flourish. After the last emphatic
chord, the players go home.

Like any other science, music is not just about making rules and
restricting one's grasp of reality to those aspects that fit the rules.
There is also an interest in contemplating natural disorderliness,
which has its own consistencies and hidden regulations. A natural
scientist takes account of the collective clamour of birds, bats, or
chirping insects, and wonders how pairing connections are established in the general mêlée. Composers in the twentieth century
have faced up to the challenge of creating alternative conditions for
music-making in which individual freedom of action is possible
within an overriding harmony. Schoenberg began by abandoning
the classical hierarchy of tonality in favour of an intuitive, later
more systematized, scheme of freely co-ordinated parts. The prob-

lem he had to solve was inadvertent consonance, and banning octave relationships was one way he hoped to avoid the distraction of unwanted harmonies. Messiaen took inspiration in the composition of complex effects modelled after birdsong. Cage devoted much of his life to compositional procedures designed to dissociate the composer's and performer's aesthetic and functional preconceptions from the musical end-product. He too faced enormous resistance from rank and file musicians all of whose training militated against independence of action and freedom of judgement. Boulez, Stockhausen, Berio, Lutosławski, late Stravinsky, and others devoted themselves to the development of serial and notational protocols designed to allow varying degrees of interpretative freedom to the conductor and individual musician.

In a paradoxical way, then, the science of harmony is interested just as much in the rules governing the isolation of individual lines of information from among a complex totality as it is concerned for the relationship of the parts to the whole. The Alpine herdsman who hangs a bell of different pitch round the neck of every cow has created a mechanism enabling him to track the movement of any chosen individual at will. It is exactly the same principle as implanting a radio transmitter on a wild animal, and just as it is vital to ensure that each transmitter sends out a clearly different signal, so the difference in pitch between one cowbell and another is also important: not only for the human observer, indeed, but for the cows themselves as badges of office (senior cows demanding the lower-pitched bells).

The criterion of harmony is satisfied here by a procedure ensuring that each member in a group has equal potential to be monitored. For radio monitoring, individual signals are organized in frequency space and enable the movement of an individual to be tracked in real time and real space. The herdsman's cattle, monitored binaurally, also signal their individual identity, location, and movement in time.

Self-evidently, the task of monitoring relatively large numbers of individuals in a group increases as the number increases. For this reason the monitoring signal has to be chosen with care to provide the required information in a minimum of time. We find it impossible, for example, to distinguish individual bees in and around a hive by their sound: first because they all buzz at around the same pitch, and second because they buzz in long bursts. Cowbells are made to be easy to hear. As musical instruments go, they are not very bright: they go pang or clunk and then the sound disappears. Of course they are designed to be heard out of doors, and not in a concert hall: cowbells monitored in a built-up environment would not perform nearly as well because their sounds would be artificially prolonged and delocalized by being reflected back and forth by floor, walls, and ceiling. For monitoring large numbers of individuals spread across a wide area, sounds of precise attack, short duration, and high frequency are best, and an absence of reverberation also helps. Natural randomness is an additional virtue. We rely on the fact that, left to their own devices, birds do not chirp in synch or cattle move in step; nor (outside the sports arena and the concert hall) does the general public spontaneously speak or sing in chorus.

Hanging cowbells on a herd of cows is an elementary example of applying musical distinctions to a practical problem with philosophical implications. They identify the herd as a group and individually. Their sounds are more easily and reliably monitored than the lowing of cattle, which remains important as an indicator of distress. Cowbells allow the herdsman freedom of movement, since the cattle can be heard from all directions and do not have to be kept continuously in view. They can also be heard in mist and fog, or poor light. Musical distinctions manifest a world as a unified and coherent acoustic space defined as multiple locations intermittently revealed.

Of course, music is more than a complex of initial distinctions. The information content of cowbell signals is space and time information relying on the invariance of pitch information from individual bells. Normal music, however, involves movement in pitch, continuous signals and superimposed layers of information. The increase in processing effort required to listen to music imposes constraints on the signalling parameters and also on the conditions of performance and listening. It means fewer pitch subdivisions and more stable pitches; fewer members in the performing ensemble and greater contrasts of timbre and manner between them; restriction of movement between the ensemble and the listening public, and restriction of space between players and audience. When we go to a concert, we pay for a fixed location, and the musicians occupy their own distinct location. They don't move and neither do we: for all the strutting and dancing of pop musicians, it doesn't affect their acoustic location in the stereo panorama.

Western classical harmony is a complex affair. For music consisting of one moving part against a static drone accompaniment, as it was for the Greeks and as it still remains for much of the world's folk music, harmony consists of regulated distinctions in pitch: the mode or scale, and the reference tone. With the arrival of polyphonic music in Western Europe, however, involving a number of musical lines moving at once, harmonic control moved from sequential tonal relationships of scale or mode to the simultaneous relationships of interval and chord. Not all pair relationships within a diatonic scale were initially permitted. In deciding which intervals and chords should be permitted, reference was made to the harmonics identified and isolated in a vibrating string with the aid of a quill or other fine implement touched lightly at different points along its length. Harmonics are a simple and effective demonstration of the existence of a hierarchy of tones in harmony with each other and with a fundamental vibration, or moving spirit, that animates everything.

Walker draws a distinction between the harmonic series, a mathematical conception, and the acoustical behaviour of a vibrating string that musicians give the name of the overtone series, and claims the overtone series to be a comparatively recent discovery. 'It is, I think, surprising that the overtones were discovered so late; one would have thought that anyone just fiddling about with a bowed instrument, let alone playing a trumpet or a tromba marina, would have hit on them . . . The existence and nature of the overtone series was only gradually being discovered during the seventeenth century by scientists such as Mersenne, Huygens and Wallis' (Walker 1978: 9, 12). I think this is overly cautious. The Pythagoreans could neither have discovered nor demonstrated the harmonic series using the monochord in any other way than by means of the overtone series: the acoustic event was the proof of the connection between mathematics and the real world. The tromba marina, so charmingly illustrated in Hans Memling's Najera panels of the 1480s, is an instrument that plays only overtones, its inadequacies in the domain of musical expression lending credence to the view that it originated as a device of acoustico-mathematical research.

There is abundant evidence, much of it circumstantial, of ancient knowledge of harmonics as overtones. In the second volume of his *Scriptores ecclesiastici de musica sacra potissimum* 1784, the Abbé Gerbert

> reproduces an ancient picture taken from a MS. at Vienna, representing 'Guido Monarchus' [Guido d'Arezzo] exhibiting his monochord to Bishop Theodaldus. He is plucking the string with the quill end of a feather, held in his left hand, while his right holds a kind of blunt knife, wherewith to stop the string at the points shown by the lettering on the body of the instrument. (Williams 1903: 75)

I take this to be a typical misinterpretation. Guido has already plucked the monochord with the unfeathered quill (not knife, its shape is plain to see), and is touching the string with the base of an uncut feather in his left hand, to produce a harmonic. The exceptional significance of the harmonic is indicated by the bishop's answering gesture of blessing, his right hand upright, with index and middle fingers raised.

The divine hierarchy extends, moreover, beyond the triune concord of first, second, and third harmonics into a populous region of closely-packed higher harmonic pitches. These orders are identified quite naturally with angels, being less powerful acoustically, and also situated at greater degrees of remoteness from the point of origin associated with the fundamental, both in terms of their physical locations as nodes on the vibrating string, and in terms of their distance as musical intervals from the fundamental pitch. Though of slighter importance, they nevertheless participate in the divine harmony.

In principle, the fundamental tone of a freely vibrating string has no 'location' on the string, since it corresponds to both fixed points—alpha and omega, as it were—of the string vibrating in its

FIG. 2. Guido d'Arezzo exhibiting his monochord to Bishop Theodaldus. The gamut inscribed advertises that the instrument is a monochord, and indicates that the harmonic being demonstrated is the note G, third harmonic of a C fundamental. This harmonic sounds an octave higher than the corresponding stopped note, which may be why Theodaldus appears so impressed. From Abbé Gerbert's *Scriptores ecclesiastici de musica sacra potissimum*, 1784.

entirety; in practice, however, string harmonics from the octave on upward are demonstrated as locations in linear sequence from one end of the string to the other, a procedure identifying the location of the fundamental as the point of origin. We recognize the same discrepancy in conflicting accounts of the creator as having no specific location, being 'omnipresent', and having a location, albeit unseen, as for example 'centre' of a concentric universe. Such apparent contradictions can be interpreted as differences in reference, aural convention focusing on the omnipresence of the fundamental, whereas visual convention, interpreting for example the observed motions of heavenly bodies as the expression of harmonic laws, having to attribute a pivotal location to the fundamental, while acknowledging the power of the centre to influence the motions of planetary bodies at a distance. In Leonardo's fresco *The Last Supper* Christ is depicted, not at the head of the table, but at its centre, a position associated with the octave or first harmonic (the table compared to a monochord).

Accounts of bishops debating how many angels are able to occupy the point of a pin have been passed down the ages as illustrations of the peculiar intellectual constructions to which medieval theology can lead. Such ideas may all the same follow rationally from the acoustic evidence of a transcendent reality in which different entities coexist in the same space. Superficially, one might interpret the debate as being about the impossibility of dealing with insubstantial entities, the point (as it were) of a pin or feather emphasizing the idea of a location without dimension as an appropriate abode for beings that do not occupy space. But the fact remains that angels were believed in, as we can see from religious paintings, so the argument is unlikely to be about the absolute reality of angels, but rather to turn on the more challenging question of the congruity of acoustic (i.e. invisible and insubstantial) and visible worlds. It seems reasonable for a medieval thinker to consider whether the positions of harmonics on a monochord are themselves strictly unreal, or anyway uncomputable, since in harmonic terms the positions represented by the two ends of the string, our alpha and omega, do in fact correspond to powers of zero and infinity, and though in terms of the physical length of the string

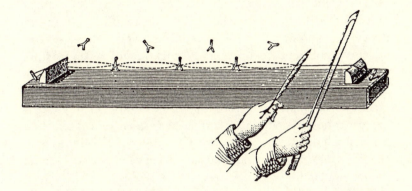

F<small>IG</small>. 3. Demonstration of harmonic nodes on the monochord using a bow and feather. The dancing objects are paper spurs placed along the string to reveal the zones of greatest and least motion. From Edgar Brinsmead, *History of the Pianoforte* (London, 1879).

harmonic nodes correspond to divisions at the half, third, fourth, fifth, and so on, in theory you cannot determine aliquot divisions on a scale of zero to infinity.

Or maybe the debate is about setting a limit to the number of harmonics admissible to the divine pantheon. This is an argument about the number of divisions in the diatonic scale. This is not; in context, a trivial matter. Legislating the notes of the scale involves assigning position and priority to pitches within the octave. Certain privileged intervals, such as the octave, fifth, and fourth, have to be respected: the intellectual problem, which is ultimately impossible to resolve in the limitations of a seven- or twelve-tone octave, lies in selecting smaller interval values that are harmonic for all possible combinations of notes in the scale. The paradox was known to the Pythagoreans and is still a matter for debate among early music specialists. It is perhaps more surprising to discover an analogous debate ongoing in the late twentieth century among a representative modern priesthood of particle physicists. String theory proposes that the material universe derives ultimately from string-like particles in continuous vibration, of which the elementary particles, or quarks, correspond to different harmonic states.

(The acoustical analogy is not always crystal clear. The 'strings' of string theory are not stretched tight, as in a musical instrument, but are loops. A musician asks how a loop is held in tension, so as to vibrate coherently, and to produce harmonics, when it is not fixed at either end. Even a rubber band has to be stretched tight between fingers or pencils, in order to sound a note of precise pitch, and string theory does not appear to allow for fixtures holding the string loop in tension. Furthermore, what kind of vibration is it that a loop can make? A normal fixed string vibration is back and forth along the string, and could be described as cyclical, though not circular.

Vibrating loops expressing harmonic relationships are normally associated with the Lissajous figures of electronic engineering, oscilloscope images of 'the path of a particle moving in a plane when the components of its position along two perpendicular axes each undergo simple harmonic motions and the ratio of their frequencies is a rational number' (Lapedes 1978: 928). But if an analogy is being made between the loops of string theory and Lissajous figures, it appears to be one between a vibrating structure and the trajectory of a mere particle.)

The contemporary equivalent to the problem of establishing how many angels are admissible to the pantheon, is that of how many harmonic states string theory may require of its fundamental string-like particles, commensurate with the number of quarks to be accounted for. For the bishops, the optimum number of notes in the scale was already fixed at seven, corresponding to the diatonic scale; the question being how to choose which harmonics to go where (given that the selection process would have to omit relatively high-ranking harmonics such as the seventh and eleventh, which despite being harmonious, are not 'in tune'). For the exponents of string theory, the number of quarks is also a reasonably settled figure that will decide how many harmonic states, or degrees of excitation, strings will have to assume for the full range of quarks to exist. This debate is not medieval superstition but the outer reaches of modern science. Both sets of bishops are bringing intelligent minds to bear on fundamental issues of the nature of the universe. 'The ontology of relativistic physics,' remarks Thomas

Kuhn, 'is, in significant respects, more like that of Aristotelian than that of Newtonian physics' (Kuhn 1993: 541).

What harmonics express in microcosm, pendulum motion expresses in the macrocosmic domain. The renewed interest in harmonics that emerges in the scientific writings of Descartes and Mersenne, and in the speculations of a Tartini, coincides with renewed research into the related phenomenon of sympathetic vibration among pendulums in scaled series. Harmonic ratios among pendulums, however, are expressed as ratios of tension or weighting, rather than linear measure, and the two are not equivalent. The point had been stated forcefully by Galilei and is restated by Mersenne in *L'Harmonie universelle* where he asks whether the octave ratio should properly be defined as 2 : 1, expressing the ratio of string length, or 4 : 1, expressing the weight ratio of pendulum motion. That the confusion is acknowledged is an indication that the two fields of enquiry were popularly intertwined (Crombie 1994: 845).

Whereas string harmonics belong to the pitch realm, pendulum motion relates to the time-scale of human actions. A correspondence can therefore be established between harmonic law as it affects the nature of creation, and laws of pendulum motion as they may determine the relationship of cycles such as the human affections. Such slow-moving frequency ratios have a bearing on the organization of musical time. Prior to the Renaissance, serious music was music for voices performing in a highly reverberant acoustic, and was geared to a voice-led scale of timing, and in some degree to the demands of text intelligibility. Late Renaissance and baroque music saw the focus of music move from the cathedral environment to the palace and the manor, and the rise of a new instrumental music aesthetic. Freed of the dual constraints of a slow-moving acoustic and the demands of language, composers and their patrons were able to indulge an interest in more secular models such as dance. The rise of the dance suite as a musical form is a feature of a renewed awareness of tempo as an expressive variable, and provided an opportunity for theorists to explore the possibility of laws for regulating tempo. As instrumental ensembles increased in size, so the need for a system of co-ordination became more urgent, and more reliant on standard notation and the guidance of a conductor or concertmaster. Different instruments have different natural tempos: horns, for example, are slow off the mark, guitars and lutes operate a dual mode of slow for chords and fast for single-line ornamental figuration, and woodwinds in general are quick. The baroque orchestra, as a large and heterogeneous collection of instruments, could no longer rely on the corporate sense of tempo associated with a consort of viols, or recorders, or other instrumental families of earlier times. With the concept of an external 'symphonic' tempo as an objective reference comes a shift of attention away from instrument-related or 'absolute' time-scales in favour of dance idioms that in addition to providing a human scale of movement, also offer a repertoire of different tempos directly relatable to particular emotions.

At the same time as the instrumental gigue, pavan, or minuet can be said to be descriptive of dance patterns and their attendant emotions, they are equally descriptive of different qualities of time-keeping—in modern terms, of information processing. A dance is about co-ordinated motion in space and time; by presenting dance forms symphonically, a composer is allowing them to be perceived objectively, and for their implications for (say) organization of labour to be understood.

The development of pendulum-based standards of musical tempo in Paris during the baroque era is further consistent with a desire, not to say a practical need, to set objective standards of musical time-keeping for mixed instrumental and vocal ensembles, standards also independent of received conventions of tempo *including* dance. With Étienne Lourié's *chronomètre*, a weighted cord that could be varied in length to oscillate more or less rapidly, a connection is made between the Greeks' experiments with pendulum motion and discovery of harmonic laws relating to motion at different frequencies, and much later experiments leading in the late eighteenth century to the invention of the metronome, which is no more than an upside-down pendulum driven by clockwork. The French inventors of pendulum timing certainly promoted their devices as a means of harmonizing the different tempos of the baroque dance suite to the same fundamental pulse (Harris-Warrick 1993: 22), and more persuasive evidence of harmonically related tempos is to be found in the high classical symphonic repertoire of Mozart, Haydn, and Beethoven.

Pendulum motion divides a time continuum into discrete packages of uniform duration. As a visual guide to timing, however, it also influences the quality of movement within the beat. Practising musicians use metronomes from an early age, and they learn from an early age that a ticking metronome is no guide at all to the quality of flow of a musical performance. The slower, majestic swing of a pendulum by contrast offers a viable image of continuous motion, and it is this model from which the baton technique of conventional conducting is clearly derived.

There is just one small problem. It is where to place the beat. Pendulum movement is a cycle of acceleration and deceleration between moments of suspended motion. It is symmetrical in time and space. The nature of pendulum movement is to be always changing: getting faster, getting slower, or momentarily still. So where does the movement start? Musicians in an orchestra have the same problem in deciding where in the course of his downbeat action the conductor intends his beat to produce a response. Pendulum motion in theory is circular motion relative to a moving observer; logically, the beat should be timed to begin at the peak of each upswing, rather than an indeterminate location on the way down. In the nature of things the peak of the upswing is a moment of rest, and arising from that, the motion of the pendulum cannot therefore be perceived as uniform, even if the timing between successive peaks is regular. Movement of a point on the circumference of a wheel goes through the same cycle of motion as a pendulum, even though the wheel itself is manifestly in uniform and continuous motion. The cycle of acceleration and deceleration within a musical beat is especially noticeable at slow tempos, and it is this image of the dynamics of pendulum slow motion that is captured in the solemn gait of French Overture style, with its characteristic dotted rhythms and surging, wave-like anacruses accelerating to successive downbeats. The image survives in French music, and not just in Debussy's *La Mer*. We recognize it today in the expressively undulatory phrasing of Boulez, now speeding up, now slowing down, now suspended in time.

On the precise correlation of pendulum motion to string vibration Mersenne seems to have had considerable doubts. Pendulums accelerate as they descend, and decelerate as they rise to a high point, and this is far from being the exact representation in slow motion of the wave motion of a stretched string, which should in principle be revealed as continuous and uniform, 'as much because the return [of motion of the pendulum] can be considered either like the violent throwing of a stone or as its natural movement towards the centre as because it has something of both, and we do not know the proportion in which the movement of missiles [or pendulums] diminishes' (Crombie 1994: 846). Mersenne's proposal to arrive at a more accurate description of string motion is to perform experiments using a string of brass or gut, not of one hundred, but one thousand feet in length, and vibrating with a periodicity of ten seconds or 0.1 hertz. The scale of magnification he envisages is impressive but not unique. Vitruvian and later Palladian principles of musical proportion in architectural interiors express a similar macroscopic conception of harmonious proportion based on actual wavelengths of various pitches. The great cathedrals of the Middle Ages, with their vastnesses of length and graven gargoyles representing the sounds of nature, are as much laboratories for acoustic experiment as places of worship, their great instruments of music the cyclotrons of a forgotten science.

11

Temperament

THE idea of dimensioning pitch in equal intervallic steps has logic on its side. In various ways, pitch can be related to length, and as length is a continuum, so one assumes is pitch also. Western studies have tended to interpret exotic scales as alternative expressions of equal temperament. A. J. Ellis, the English translator of Helmholtz's *On the Sensations of Tone* and an indefatigable annotator of non-Western scales—as embodied in museum collections of wind and percussion instruments—promoted the view that equal divisions of the octave should be taken as the norm, leading the musicologist Carl Stumpf in 1901 to wonder how the Siamese were supposed to derive an equal-tempered seven-tone scale without the help of logarithm and square root tables (Schneider and Beurmann 1993: 198–9).

Back in the early 1980s I was working on computer programs to compose and harmonize melodies. (The results are summarized in the next chapter.) My computer was an early Apple IIE with limited memory, so the program was designed to assign pitches as well as deciding the movement of a melody from note to note. The onboard music chip was set up with a default range of pitches an equal-tempered quarter-tone apart, called up by consecutive numbers. To generate pitches in the twelve-tone chromatic scale all a programmer had to do was ensure that the number values ultimately converted to melody and harmony were either all odd or all even: that way you avoided quarter-tones.

My interest eventually turned to the classic diatonic major and minor scales. These are not even-step scales like the chromatic scale. There are seven notes in the octave rather than twelve, and they are organized in irregular groups of tones and semitones. The successive notes in a scale are called degrees: unison, second, third, fourth, fifth, sixth, seventh, octave. A musical interval is also defined in degrees of a diatonic scale: a third is a span of three notes, a fifth, of five notes. A musical melody is defined for the purpose of the program as a succession of moves between pitches corresponding to degrees of a chosen scale. In programming a computer to compose a melody I originally began by generating numbers in succession, positive and negative, corresponding to upward or downward intervals in semitones, to be added to the value of the immediately preceding note. This produced a melody wandering at random over the keyboard, since it had no programmed allegiance to any one key. The new idea was to treat successive numbers as degrees of a pre-ordained scale: this would ensure that the melody stayed firmly in a particular key, and could therefore easily be transposed to a different key, and converted from major to minor, or vice versa.

As major and minor scales are not evenly spaced divisions of the octave, to achieve that goal one would normally have to think of incorporating a subroutine to convert degrees of the scale into pitch values set up to allow for the discrepancies between tone and semitone divisions. For various reasons I disliked the idea of having look-up tables for pitch conversion. On the practical side they would occupy scarce memory, and would slow down operation of the program. But look-up tables were also an inelegant solution. I wanted to see if a formula could be found to convert equal fractions of an octave into appropriate major or minor scales when the result of successive aggregations was rounded down to the nearest chromatic note value. I wanted to end up with a method of specifying a melody in degrees of a scale such that a sequence starting from base middle C and expressed as values 1, 2, 3, 4, and 5 in succession would be reproduced chromatically as the note sequence C, C♯, D, D♯, E; or alternatively in C major as C, D, E, F, G; or in C minor as C, D, E♭, F, G.

In *The Concept of Music* I explained how by trial and error fractional values were found that converted into major and minor scales in the production of synthetic melodies. The fractional value producing a minor scale turned out to be smaller than that producing a major scale. There is an apparent contradiction here: surely an octave is an octave, whether divided into major or minor, so how is it possible to have two seven-tone equal-tempered scales of different interval sizes? The answer is that each added interval being rounded down to the nearest semitone in effect allows the octave an extra semitone of possible expansion to cater for seventh degrees on the larger side. As musical intonation is not an exact science, such freedom to adjust intervals is perfectly acceptable in practice.

The interesting implication of major and minor scales corresponding to compromise applications of wider and narrower subdivisions of the octave is that the emotional associations of different scales can be linked to their underlying interval size. After further investigations, a further range of interval values was discovered that produced useful approximations to the Greek modes, ranging from the narrow tone step of the Aeolian mode to the extremely wide interval characteristic of the Phrygian mode.

The determination of intervals in a musical scale is known as its temperament. The words *scale* and *temperament* link concepts of measurement (scale as in 'scale drawing'), emotional character ('temper'), and inner strength (as in 'tempered steel'). The idea of different modes corresponding to different emotions is widespread in the history and practice of music, and was certainly firmly accepted by the Greek philosophers. In relating modal characters to degrees of expansion or contraction of intervals within the octave, one can identify the association of mode and emotional type as having a rational basis and not merely as custom and practice. For a stringed instrument such as the lyre, whose strings are tuned to the prevailing mode, the choice of mode affects the tension of the strings. The greater the step size, the more the string has to be tightened, and the brighter its tone. A mode of smaller interval size will tend to sound relatively subdued, and where the interval size is large, it will sound with greater brilliance and resonance.

In studying ancient writings on music it is as well to recognize the acoustic model on which a particular theory is based. In asking the question (in *De anima*) whether it is the thing struck or the striker that makes the sound (gives a sound its identifiable pitch and

timbre), Aristotle is taking percussion as his model of sound production. We can conceptualize Aristotle's sound world as a music
box, or in today's language, a synthesizer. It is a sound world of
exact tonal relationships brought into play by human (or divine)
will and theoretically incapable of encompassing individual performer intention or emotion. Aristotle is challenged by Avicenna,
who describes an alternative model of sound production by the
forcible squeezing of air between two bodies that may be either soft
or hard. This alternative model corresponds to the voice (air forced
between the folds of the larynx), or the lips (for a trumpet or horn),
or the blades of grass that make the single and double reeds of
woodwind instruments (Burnett 1991: 52–3)—or indeed, the
musical world of M. Le Petomane, who played tunes by expressing air from his anal sphincter (Nohain and Caradec 1992). A sound
world based on the lip-reed model is significantly different from
Aristotle's mechanistic conception. It embraces sound production
as intentional and capable of manipulation for effect; it also assumes
the principle of continuity of action for note production, in contrast to percussion, which relies on initiation only. The focus of
Avicenna's sound world is inescapably bound up with human
actions and emotions. Boethius' famously erroneous account of
hearing musical intervals in the pitches sounded by different-sized
blacksmith's hammers signals a reversion to Aristotle's percussion
model, but (one suspects) primarily as a means of adding credibility to observations concerning pitch relationships in plucked
strings. Unlike Aristotle, Boethius recognizes duration as an aspect
of musical pitch, a perception more appropriate to the sound of
plucked strings than to hammers, whose sounds simply ping on the
anvil and then vanish. (Duration is understood as the time taken for
a sound to decay after it has been initiated. The time-span of a
sound sustained by continuous excitation, by breath for example,
in singing or playing a wind instrument, or by bow action in the
case of a string instrument, is not 'duration' in this sense, since the
sound produced is constantly in a state of beginning.)

There are two distinct classes of plucked string instrument acting
as models for the Greek philosophers of music. For Pythagoras, the
model was the harp; for Plato, the lyre or kithara, instruments of

more robust construction, modelled on the horned skull of a bull or deer, supporting a limited number of strings of similar length tuned to a mode. Each string corresponds to a note in a fixed scale. The instrument belongs in partnership with the player's voice. The lyre provides the correct pitch cues, to which the singer's voice adds human qualities of reverberation, attenuation, emotional resonance, and also language. The juxtaposition of human frailties and uncertainties of intonation with the fixed intonation of the lyre captures the relationship of the humanly possible and the divinely ordained.

What holds the body together, and so keeps it 'in tension', is the right mixture, or *harmonia*, of hot, cold, etc.—and this right mixture or *harmonia* is the soul. What Simmias seems to mean here [in his commentary on Plato's *Phaedo*] is that 'having a soul' (being ensouled or alive) is merely another way of describing the state of the bodily constituents when mixed and 'in tension' . . . a precise parallel to the case of the lyre: there, as here, the relevant state arises simply as a result of the adjustment of physical elements. (C. J. Rowe, in Plato 1993: 205)

Temperance is a central consideration in Plato's discussion of good government in *The Republic*. The state being good, he says, is wise, brave, temperate, and just. Wisdom is defined as residing in the management of skills in relation one to another, and in the conduct of the commonwealth as a functioning body of parts, internally and in relation to other states. The musical analogy is of performing the instrument of state so that its various strings make concord together (internal relations), and so that it resounds effectively as an example to others (external relations). Courage is linked to endurance (duration), and thus to the quality of manufacture of the instrument of state. Plato seizes on the remarkable and unusual analogy of permanent colour in dyed wool, whose lasting attributes are due to human science and industry applied to natural products rather than to strength of individual character or volition. Far from being an expression of individual actions or underlying emotions, courage is a sign of workmanship 'never to be washed out by pleasure and pain, desire and fear, solvents more terribly effective than all the soap and fuller's earth in the world'.

Temperance addresses the tuning of the instrument of state, representing the body politic, and at the human level, the balance of organic functions within the individual body. It 'extends throughout the whole gamut of the state, producing a consonance of all its elements from the weakest to the strongest, as measured by any standard you like to take. . . . So we are entirely justified in identifying with temperance this unanimity or harmonious agreement between the naturally superior and inferior elements.' (IV. 431)

The tuning or temperament of a lyre is expressed as a mode. On Plato's choice of ideal mode, the dialogue is instructive:

What are the modes that express sorrow?

—Modes like the Mixed Lydian [*sic*] and the Hyperlydian [Mixolydian step size: 0.85 tone].

Which are the modes expressing softness and the ones used at drinking-parties?

—There are the Ionian and certain Lydian modes which are called 'slack' [Ionian step size: 0.88 tone; Lydian 0.86].

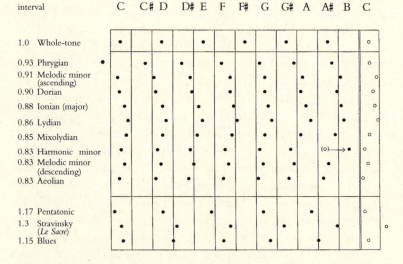

FIG. 4. Modes.

Note: The diagram illustrates how different modes and scales may arise from tuning the divisions of the seven-note octave to wider or narrower equidistant intervals and aurally compensating to fit the resulting notes into a pattern of standard harmonious pitches.

Source: Maconie 1990.

(Desmond Lee, in the current Penguin edition, renders 'slack' as 'languid', which has the merit of greater intelligibility but at the cost of sacrificing any sense of a connection between human behaviour and the imagery of the lyre and its tuning.)

You will not use them in the training of your warriors?

—Certainly not. You seem to have [only] the Dorian and Phrygian left.

I am not expert in these modes, I said; but leave me one which will fittingly represent the tones and accents of a brave man in warlike action, who . . . will meet every blow of fortune with steadfast endurance [Phrygian step size: 0.93 tone, Dorian 0.90].

—These two modes you must leave; the two which will best express the accents of courage in the face of stern necessity and misfortune, and of temperance in prosperity.

The modes you want, he replied, are just the two I mentioned.

—Our songs and airs, then, will not need instruments of large compass capable of modulation into all the modes, and we shall not maintain craftsmen to make them, in particular the flute, which has the largest compass of all. That leaves the lyre and the kithara for use in the town; and in the country the herdsmen may have some sort of pipe. (III. 398–9)

When Plato speaks of a harmonious agreement among naturally superior and inferior elements of the population, the musical analogy is evidently not as we would understand it, as a harmony of chords and chord progressions made up of notes of equal status, but rather refers to pitch relationships within a scale of notes of variable status. The determination of status of a note is its relative pitch. Higher notes have higher status because of their higher degree of tension, lower notes lower status because of their lower degree of tension within the mode. A mode is thus not only graded degrees of pitch, but degrees of pitch that signify graded degrees of tension or steadfastness. The analogy is only true of instruments such as the lyre and kithara, whose strings are all of the same length; it is not true of the harp, whose strings are of different length, but all of the same tension. In the harp, every note expresses the same degree of steadfastness, so there can be no implication of higher status for higher pitches. (Plato appears contemptuous of woodwinds such as the shepherd's pan-pipes, and by implication the aulos favoured by courtesans, objecting perhaps to instruments that do not suit his analogy of tension and temperament, and that are associated with classes of society that act in accordance with the baser instincts of humankind. Flutes also do not conform to the ideal of harmony with the (male) voice range, being high in pitch, like the voices of women and children.)

Maintaining a range of strings at different tensions places the fabric of an instrument under considerable and unequal strain. On the high-pitched side, there will be an excess of tension, and on the low-pitched side, a shortage of tension. To withstand these unequal stresses the build of the instrument has to be solid, and solidity makes for a less singing or resonant structure (compared, for example, with the harp, or with later instruments such as the lute, violin family, or guitar, whose strings, grouped along a central fingerboard, allow the different stresses to be adequately distributed throughout a lightweight frame and more efficient resonating chamber). In theory, the strings of a lyre are of the same material and gauge, but at different degrees of tension, giving rise to different tone qualities, the lower strings sounding duller and the higher strings brighter. In practice, as with the modern guitar and violin, one chooses thicker and coarser strings for the lower pitches, and thinner and stronger strings for the higher. From a Platonic viewpoint there is nothing much between the two: the poor old lower strings are either 'thick', or they are 'dull', in comparison with the progressively more highly strung remainder. Society, says Plato, is like that: the thick and the dull coexisting in a harmonious gamut along with the brave and highly-strung.

That is the difference between Plato and Pythagoras. Plato's scale is a scale of tensions that correspond to degrees of physical and emotional strength, and when we consider Plato on music, it is in relation to individual virtuosity (a combination of physical tech-nique and elevated character) and the control and expression of human emotion. For Pythagoras, however, the musical scale is about linear measure. The divisions of a monochord, indicating the positions of octave and other harmonic relationships, are constant whatever the tuning or tension of the monochord may be. Instruments embodying measure are the harp and related instru-ments of the zither and harpsichord families. These instruments in general are of unrestricted range: there is no voice-related restriction to two octaves that is part and parcel of the lyre/kithara philosophy. Harps can be high or low in pitch without carrying the burden of suggestion of mood-swinging between high and low, and are therefore more appropriate instruments for heavenly angels, who are above human emotions and whose music represents pure (i.e. numerical) relationships.

Augustine, when he discussed Psalm 42.4–5 in his *Enarrationes in Psalmos*, turned his attention to . . . why it is that the psalmist sometimes gives praise on the cithara, sometimes on the psaltery. . . . Both instruments are carried in the hand; both are struck; both make sounds pleasing to the deity. But the sounding box of the psaltery is located on the upper part of the instrument, that of the cithara on the lower. Herein lies the distinction. When we obediently carry out God's commandments, an activity involving no suffering, it is the psaltery that plays. But when we suffer tribulation—that suffering which comes *ex inferiore parte*, because we are mortal—then it is the cithara. (Sears 1991: 22)

One can trace the history of Western keyboard instruments as a continuous oscillating between Pythagorean and Platonic ideals: the objective, even-toned plucked spinet yielding to the more expressive clavichord, responsive to finger pressure, as later the uniformly strung eighteenth-century fortepiano of the classical Enlightenment era was superseded in the nineteenth century by the pianoforte, more solidly built to withstand the higher stresses of stringing varying from thick single strings in the bass to thin multiple strings in the treble, and designed to suit a Romantic aesthetic of emotional tension.

The same can be said of guitar construction in the twentieth century, the solid-bodied electric guitar representing a reversion, in construction and symbolism, to the ancient Greek lyre/kithara ideal. The rise to fame in the 1970s of the solid-bodied electric guitar, colloquially named 'the axe', coincided with a newly heroic pop music aesthetic of extravagant musical action and aggressive posturing of singers and lead guitarists operating at the higher extremes of vocal pitch and instrumental intensity. To make it easier for players to reach the high end of the fingerboard, the traditional rounded guitar body was modified by cut-outs that in certain models make the instrument visually resemble a lyre.

Not only was society regulated by tensions. Heraclitus had long since proposed that matter too was organized in a scale of energy states from low to high. He saw the variety of creation in terms of degrees of tension between limits that he called 'earth' and 'fire', but that we would now call states ofinertia and radiation, or even 'particle' and 'wave'. The stability of the elements is explained in harmonic terms, as tension ratios representing steady states.

The doctrine of *Opposite Tension* which Heraclitus applied to the inter-pretation of nature was derived, as his own words inform us, from his observation of the state of the string in the bow and the lyre. According to Heraclitus there is in things a force that moves them on the Upward Path to Fire, and an opposite force that moves them on the Downward Path to Earth. The existence of matter in any particular state is the result of a balance of opposing forces, of Tension. Even the most stable things in appearance are the battleground of opposing forces, and their stability is only relative. [Nature's] mode of existence is an eternal oscillation between these two extremes. (Harrington 1961: 40)

It is startling to think of Heraclitus in the fifth century BC defining the elements as modes of oscillation between matter and energy. That is a measure of the power of the acoustical model to account for catastrophic changes of state, such as melting and evaporation, as well as the absence of change characteristic of elements in a steady state, as expressions of oscillatory motion. Change presup-poses motion, that is clear; the insight is to conceive a steady state in nature in the terms of a musical tone, which is constant and unchanging by virtue of continuous motion within conditions of consistent tension.

We have to be careful in distinguishing an arbitrary scale of values between two extremes from a scale of values expressing har-monic ratios. An arbitrary scale is the kind represented by Plato's modes, which correspond to human value systems rather than to laws of harmonic vibration. In order to validate a particular choice of mode one has to establish by argument or ingenuity that it is sanctified by the laws of acoustics. This Plato does not do: he is content to make an intellectual point. Others after him were anx-ious to reconcile the human politics of musical temperament with the divinely ordained values of harmonic ratios: hence the endless research, culminating in the great controversies of the sixteenth and seventeenth centuries, into alternative systems of tuning.

Those without practical musical experience can fall victim to confusion between the revealed truths of intervallic measures and harmonics as locations on a stretched string, and the humanly ordained divisions representing tempered tuning. The idea of a hierarchy of tensions as propounded by Plato and Heraclitus is not automatically equivalent to the hierarchy of harmonics observed by Pythagoras, which do not express differences in tension at all, though the interval values they express are used as a means of regulating degrees of tension. We recognize the difference between music played on a violin first in harmonics, then in normal fingering. The first is ethereal, other-worldly; the second is real, and able to convey emotion. As a geometer, Pythagoras had no use for tension *per se*: his primary interest was in correlating pitch and length, which can only be done reliably if string tension is a constant. Unlike Plato, Pythagoras would not discriminate against women and children merely because their voices were 'less heroic' in temper, at the same pitch, than adult male voices; conceivably, that makes Pythagoras more of a democrat.

The same confusion of harmonics and temperament continues to surface in modern physics where acoustic and musical images are borrowed without understanding of their full implications. Superstring theory seeks to account for the ultimate building blocks of matter. In its original form the theory expresses particle differences in terms surprisingly resonant of Heraclitus' theory of tensions. 'Quarks interact through the inter-quark force. One can envisage the bonds produced by this force as being pieces of elastic joining the quarks. Indeed, the inter-quark force shares with elastic the property that it grows [i.e. the tension increases] with distance. As the quarks cavort about so the interactions within the hadron resemble a whirling string. Under these circumstances the "elastic" is more important to the dynamics than the quarks on the end of it' (Davies and Brown 1988: 68).

I have some trouble with this analogy. Certainly, the force available to drive an arrow increases as the arrow is drawn and the tension of the string increases, the increase in tension expressed as a rise in audible pitch of the string in consequence of its resistance to the force applied. The length of a bowstring does not change as it is drawn, and therein lies its efficiency as a source of energy. But elastic is different. It stretches as it is pulled, and the consequence of it getting longer as force is applied is that its audible pitch remains virtually constant no matter how much it is pulled, or at least until it breaks. So it is difficult to imagine how the energy potential available to a hadron through an elastic inter-quark force would actually increase with distance. For the parallel to be exact the 'pitch' of a quark pair would have to be determined by what the distance between the quarks was at the outset, not by anything that happened later on, just as the twang of an elastic band is determined by its length at rest, and not by any degree of stretch it may sustain at any other time. The authors claim the elasticity of the bond to be more important to the dynamics of the inter-quark relationship than the quarks at either end. But their analogy appears to say exactly the opposite, that the energy potential remains the same whatever the distance.

The earlier Heraclitan/Platonist view of variable tension as the distinguishing characteristic is superseded by an alternative Pythagorean view of harmonic excitation as the operative variable responsible for the altered states of matter (see the previous chapter). Acoustically speaking, it is one or the other and cannot be both. Either tension is the variable, in which case the quarks are related in an arbitrary 'temperament', or harmonic excitation is the variable, in which case tension is a constant and the quarks express different states of excitation of a common fundamental vibration.

12

Melos

PLATO required of melody that it consist of fixed and distinct pitches, be fit for singing, and noble in character. An approved melody is sung in tune and without deviating from the chosen mode; it respects the compass of the singing voice, and expresses the character consistent with the mode. Noises and gliding pitches (portamenti) are forbidden, extremes of range (which may distort voice quality) are discouraged, and a discriminating choice of mode (the heroic modes referred to in *The Republic*) is to be preferred. Plato regarded melody as an abstract ideal, in contrast to Aristoxenus, for whom melody was a natural form of expression to be rationally investigated. Plato's attention is focused on the system within which a melody may be free to act; Aristoxenus is more concerned with the human motives that lead to expression in melody, and thus to the dynamics of a musical line. 'Virtually all Aristoxenus's harmonic laws are expressed as rules of progression' (Barker 1991: 152).

One way of coming to terms with these elusive but sophisticated perceptions is to begin from ground zero, as it were, and try to find what makes a melody tick, or rather glide. Programming a computer to compose melody involves inventing rules of note selection that may help us to understand what Plato and Aristoxenus are talking about. A computer has no scruples and no preconceptions. It relies on a program. For a program to be successful the computer must be allowed some freedom of choice, otherwise it could hardly be said to invent the melodies it produces. Equally, certain musical preconditions must be set if the resulting invention is to be recognized as a plausible melody, and not just a string of notes. From this viewpoint Plato represents a reductionist approach that enables a melody program to be devised, and Aristoxenus the anthropological approach that enables the resulting melodies to be authenticated.

A melody is first and foremost a movement in pitch. The movement is expressed in terms of a scale or mode, but can be recognized as the same when the scale or mode is transposed from a high to a low key, or changed from major to minor, and even when compressed into a smaller interval with microtonal inflections:

Werner showed that people were able to recognize melodies when they were transformed on to extremely small scales, so that the interval sizes were grossly distorted. Furthermore, White found that melodies were recognized with fair accuracy when all the interval sizes were set to one semitone, leaving only the direction of pitch change. (Deutsch 1977: 112)

The whole concept of 'out-of-tuneness' of melody is fascinating and paradoxical. There is no logical reason why melodies should be recognized as out-of-tune rather than in-tune-but-different, other than that somehow we recognize pitch ratios for music only as part of recognizing a melody, a more important feature being the direction of movement. Similar perceptions apply to the interpretation of the inflection patterns of ordinary speech. Phoneticians employ a simplified notation for speech melody as pitch and intensity cues within a two-line stave representing top and bottom of the voice range, acknowledging that absolute pitch values do not apply, rather the melody of a speaker's voice is perceived in relation to a notional range of pitch variation that is specific to the individual. Within that 'organic range' however, a narrow band or 'paralinguistic range' is identifiable as a pitch-setting chosen to convey attitude or intention (in music, 'tessitura'). A third variable is the degree of natural volatility in a speaker's conversational speech, which is a matter of individual temperament and may also be culturally determined (Laver 1994: 456–7).

Melody forms also abound, from the medieval *estampie* via classical variations to jazz, and from the literate musical cultures of the West to the oral musical cultures of Africa, the Middle East, and Asia, which are based on the idea of progressive elaboration and distortion of a standard melody shape. These alterations are recognized as versions of the same model, even though they may be divested of virtually every outwardly recognizable feature of the original, like Picasso's painted variations on Velázquez. Evidently melody is able to capitalize on some aspect of the listening process that senses underlying affinities at a level of intention or implication.

Research into computer-generated melody has typically been directed at the derivation of operational rules of melody sequence from analysis of existing melodies, whether a fragment of Mozart, or Webern, or a folk-song. The computer derives a set of rules (loaded probabilities) of where a melody is likely to go next based on where it has come from, and then composes further sequences 'in the style', or according to the same balances of probabilities. The new melodies are compared with the original and the more plausible they are, the better the rules are supposed to be. An alternative approach is to avoid aesthetic rules altogether, and simply establish the essential conditions for melody production, that is to say operational rather than aesthetic rules, letting the computer get on with the job. A minimalist approach is endorsed to some extent by the profile method of melody classification developed by Denys Parsons for his *Directory of Tunes and Musical Themes* (1975). Searching for a more economical and versatile alternative to Kobbé's famous directory of opera themes, Parsons discovered that by encoding a melody simply as a sequence of directional changes expressed as permutations of up (U), down (D), and repeated note (R), it was possible to identify a particular melody (more accurately, a melody beginning or incipit) in as few as a dozen characters. As an *aide-mémoire* for people who cannot read music, his method takes advantage of the fact that people are usually able to remember the up-and-down motion of a melody even if they are unable to say what key it is in, or what are its precise notes, rhythms, or intervals. A system that works at this fundamental level of awareness may be telling us something about the origins of melody creation as well as perception (Parsons 1992: 144; see also Cerulo 1992: 111–29).

We begin with the proposition that a melody is a fluctuation of pitch (singular) and not a loose succession of notes. That is already saying something about the way a melody is organized and programmed, as well as possibly something about the way in which it is perceived. There is room for both alternatives, the single ribbon as well as the 'string of beads' option, but it is more profitable initially to proceed on the assumption that a melody is the discontinuous expression of a continuous curve.

The determining parameters of a melody, leaving aside for the time being factors such as note duration, rhythm, and dynamics, are scale, interval, range, and a fourth ingredient, 'bounce', that comes into play when the rise or fall of a melody leads to an extreme of range beyond which the voice or instrument cannot comfortably go, and acts to turn the direction of the melody back toward the middle range.

Plato's dictum that melody is properly vocal, and his disdain for purely instrumental music (the pan-pipes, for instance), is an acknowledgement that in addition to a consciousness of extremes of range, the singer is also aware of an intermediate zone within which a melody may fix on a point of departure and to which it may return. Instruments do not have that natural median pitch to act as a position of rest, a fulcrum or pivot point against which a melody movement can be judged. Both Plato and Aristoxenus are agreed on the meaning of melody as residing in the elaboration of tensions expressed in the rise and fall of the voice, a perception central to the Platonic requirement of imitation.

The whole of the discussion of correctness [in *Laws* 668B–C] turns upon it. So too, for instance, does his rejection of purely instrumental music as an acceptable form of art, on the grounds that if it is music it must be *mimesis* but that in the absence of words 'it is impossibly difficult to understand what it means, and what worthwhile imitation it is like' (*Laws* 669E). (Barker 1991: 141)

Being conceived for a musical instrument of indeterminate range, computer-generated melody has no natural *mese* or median pitch, and 'bounce' therefore is a deliberately artificial device to keep it safely within bounds.

A scale or mode can be described as the degree of resolution of a continuous musical line, for example pentatonic, diatonic, chromatic, or microtonal (i.e. 5, 7, 12, or more than 12 notes to the octave). Exceptionally, it may be defined as a harmonic series, for a bugle or natural horn melody. The simplest option for a melody program is one allowing melodic movement to all notes of the chromatic scale.

The voice is a one-note instrument that can change its pitch. Other musical instruments are multiple-note devices that allow for the selection of one note (sometimes more) at a time. The difference is crucial when we come to consider how a melody program is implemented. Logically, a melody can be described as a succession of pitches, and to implement a program one has only to instruct the computer to select at random from a data file of numbers corresponding to pitches within the chosen range. That amounts in essence to the keyboard approach, and it produces random melodies much as a child picks out notes at random on a piano keyboard. The alternative approach is based on Parsons's principle of movement up or down in relation to the previous note, and a melody by this definition is a succession of intervals in additive progression. An interval is a numerical value, either positive or negative, in semitonal units. A zero value interval is realized as a repeated note. The range of a melody is defined by how far it may rise and fall in pitch from the highest to the lowest note, a consideration traditionally related to the voice or instrument for which a melody is composed. By defining a melody as the distance travelled from note to note, a degree of consistency is assured in the melody overall, related to a notional degree of flexibility of the voice or instrument, and related to that, what might be recognized as a notional idiomatic quality: 'the nature of melos is revealed in principles governing the form of movement from place to place. Further, . . . its arrival at a certain place by a given route carries implications for the nature of its subsequent progress' (Barker 1991: 158).

The melody program is therefore able to influence the continuity of flow of a randomly generated melody by limiting the size of interval a melody may rise or fall in a single step. If the vocal norm is taken to be plainchant, or the melody from *Neighbours*, the range of step size will be relatively small. Classical music for solo voice does not always correspond to this easy relaxed idiom. 'In Bach's music', said Debussy, 'it is not the character of the melody that stirs us, but rather the tracing of a particular line . . . No-one has ever been known to whistle Bach' (Debussy 1962: 23). What Debussy means is that Bach's melodies are too broken, too instrumental in character to suit the taste of a French composer of the flute melody to *L'Après-midi d'un faune*. The rise of classical instrumental music in the baroque era from Vivaldi through Bach and Handel, is marked by a liberation in melody writing for the voice away from a traditional moderation of interval movement toward imitation of the more robust flexibility and agility of orchestral instruments, such as the oboe and trumpet, a new interpretation of traditional mimesis that reaches a peak perhaps with the two-octave-plus leaps and incandescently high register of the Queen of the Night's 'Vengeance' aria in Mozart's *The Magic Flute*. For present purposes, however, the program operates within self-evidently vocal limitations. We want the melody to stay within bounds, and this means setting up a detection loop within the program. The simplest mechanism works on the rigid barrier principle, so that when the melody drifts to the very top or bottom of its range, the program assumes that the balance of choice is unfairly weighted and acts to correct it so the melody will tend to move back in the opposite direction. In practice a melody drifting to either extreme of range may stick for some time before the change of balance takes effect to make it drift back toward the centre.

To establish the optimum starting conditions for creating a plausible melody, we start with minimum conditions: a one-octave range, and a maximum interval step up or down of one semitone. A random melody under these restrictions tends to oscillate in slow motion from one extreme in pitch to the other. It has features consistent with speech monologue, meaning enough variation in pitch to avoid a continuous monotone, but not enough variation in interval to suggest meaningful interpretation or emotion, and may be compared with the voice inflection of someone reading a text who has no idea of what it means.

By increasing the choice of interval from one to three semitones, a maximum of a minor third up or down, a more pleasing melodic effect is created, bearing some idiomatic resemblances to Middle Eastern chant. Such a prescription is closely matched by Ravel's celebrated theme from *Bolero*, both in its type of flow and in its tendency to stick at extremes of range. In this case the melody (expressed for ease of reading in the key of C) begins with a long note that turns out to lie near the top of the range, and its subsequent movement indicates a probability weighting in favour of a gradual descent to the C an octave lower. Intervals greater than a tone are shown in brackets:

C − − B C D C B [A C − C A C] − − B [C A] [G E] F G − −
F E D E F G A G − − A B A G F E D E D C − −

—at which point Ravel's compositional program introduces a change of direction or 'bounce' that has the effect of reversing a gradual downward trend into a dramatic upward climb by leaps and bounds:

C D E [F D − G] − − − etc.

—leading by a further leap of a fifth to the D at the top of the melody range from which the answering melody begins:

[(G) D] − − C B A B C D C B − − [A C] B [A F] − F F [F −
A] − [C A] [B G] F − F F [F − A] − [B G] [A F D] − D C D −
− D C D E F G − − F E D C etc.

In this answering melisma Ravel's maximum permitted interval size is subtly increased from a minor to a major third. It sounds more relaxed; the range remains the same (an octave and a tone), and the melody still tends to drift in a downward direction and continues to stick at extremes of range.

The angle of drift of a melody can be shallow or steep. It will be shallow if consecutive intervals are generally small, and steep if they tend to be larger in size. The folk-song 'Danny Boy' is an example of a melody with a higher proportion of larger intervals within the range up to a fourth. The combination of larger interval sizes and 'two-handed' up-down symmetries ('the pipes | the pipes' . . . 'from glen to glen | And down the mountain side') suggesting origins as a harp melody:

B C D E − − D [E A] [G E] D [C A] − − [C E] F G − − A [G
E C E] [D − − B] C D E − − etc. (Ex.1.(*a*))

This melody also has a tendency to stick at extremes of range: the lower A, and the upper G. Yet another example is the melody

'Jerusalem' composed by Parry to Blake's poem beginning 'And did those feet in ancient time'; this melody is interesting because it tends to move upward by large interval steps, and descend by small interval steps:

[C E G][A – – C] A G F G – – – A G F [G E] D – [C – A] etc. (Ex.1.(*b*))

Ex. 1.   (a) 'O Danny Boy'; (b) 'Jerusalem'

(*a*)

etc.

(*b*)

etc.

In programming terms, the sawtooth shape arises when a melody program is inherently biased in favour of movement in one direction, and also when the 'bounce' over-compensates in favour of movement in the reverse direction. As the above examples show, this imbalance can nevertheless lead to aesthetically pleasing results (the opening violin theme of the Mozart G minor Symphony discussed elsewhere in Chapter 16 is also 'sawtooth' in shape).

A randomly generated melody incorporating range and bounce conditions can be understood as a continuous composite curve influenced by three separate oscillations:

(i)   fluctuations of note-to-note interval size within a chosen bandwidth;

(ii) a slower oscillation back and forth between upper and lower extremes of range; and

(iii) an oscillation of bounce, that is, of the probability of melodic movement up or down.

Though triggered by the melody reaching an extreme of range, the bounce oscillation is not necessarily in step with or in parallel with the curve of a melody. After a melody has settled down, bounce will also eventually settle down into a weak oscillation between particular plus or minus values, or in certain instances, around a particular plus or minus value. The amplitude and frequency of bounce oscillation will vary as the melody range and interval parameters are varied, and is further influenced, as will be seen, according to the mode of range-sensing built into the program. If the program instructs a melody to stick at an extreme of range until sufficient bounce has accumulated to dislodge it, a slow climb may well be followed by a sudden and precipitous drop, or vice versa. Where there is excess bounce a melody may deteriorate into a forced pendulum oscillation between extremes of range.

The description of a melody as a dynamical system allows interesting parallels to be drawn with other examples in nature of complex periodicities:

The Italian mathematician Vito Volterra (1860–1940) devised a simple model of the populations of predators and food fish in the Mediterranean sea. He was trying to explain a curious observation made by the biologist Umberto D'Ancona: during the First World War, when the amount of fishing decreased, the catches contained a greater percentage of predators. Volterra found the reason: the populations fluctuated periodically, in a manner that on average was to the predators' advantage . . . The periodicity is essentially a consequence of delays in the response of the component populations. Imagine that the population of prey is high, but that of predators is low. Predators will then increase, depleting the food supply. Because of the relatively slow reproductive rate of predators, however, the population of predators will tend to overshoot the level that the food can sustain. Now the predator population drops, but until it becomes very low, the prey cannot increase substantially. Once there are few enough predators, however, there is a rapid explosion of the faster-reproducing food fish, and the cycle starts anew. (Stewart 1993: 31–2)

Normally, of course, a melody doesn't bob up to the top of its range and wait there, like a toy diver at the surface of a glass of water. It isn't normal because extremes of range are normally difficult for voices and instruments to reach (this remains true even of keyboard instruments). Real melodies tend therefore to veer away some distance short of their limits of range, or when they do not, as at climaxes, to prepare for a top or bottom note by a change of rate of ascent or descent. The question is how to change the program's response to an interval value that would take the melody outside the prescribed range. In its simplest form it detects whether the next note is going to be higher or lower than the range allows, and if so substitutes the appropriate limit value. This effectively pins the melody to its extreme while the bounce subroutine takes effect. A variation of the program causes the offending interval to be cancelled outright instead of being guillotined to fit; the effect of allowing the melody to pause over a range of pitches up to the extreme values is a more natural sounding flow, allowing a melody line to rise to a range of peaks of various heights instead of to a level plateau.

As one continues to experiment by increasing the interval step and melody range limits, the character of a synthetic melody can be heard to change from a relatively smooth vocal style to a more jagged instrumental style, and from a modal to a more diatonic idiom. One is aware of the progressive expansion of melodic contour as a virtual advance in historical terms to an idiom recognizably closer to the twentieth-century expressionism of a vocal line out of Berg's *Wozzeck* or even to Boulez's *Le Marteau sans maître*. To achieve the ultimate distinction of a melody in pointillist idiom, however, the note-to-note permitted interval range has to be measured in octaves rather than semitones. A fair approximation to Xenakis is achieved if the interval range is in excess of six octaves, when more notes fall outside the chosen range (and are replaced by silence) than are caught within. Xenakis's pioneering use of the computer as a composing medium makes this aesthetic coincidence hardly surprising; indeed, it is arguably an example of mimesis of an unexpected but theoretically approved kind.

Up to this point we have been proceeding on the basis that a melody is the discontinuous expression of a single continuous curve. This may be the case for a great many types of melody, but it is not the entire story. In the Western European tradition, melody is affected simultaneously by harmony and harmonic movement. Affinities between successive notes of a classical tonal melody are created not only by convenient proximity, but also by common membership of triadic harmonies, related in turn to underlying structures of key relationship. To do justice to established conventions of harmony and tonal progression in melody synthesis requires programming of some complexity, entailing the implication that natural melodies are not really free at all. A number of attempts have been made to incorporate textbook rules of harmony into composition software, to ensure that melodies are properly tonal. Such programs may indeed produce reasonable melodies: the question is whether they can be seriously described as spontaneous inventions. The paradox is that ordinary people without formal training in rules of harmony nevertheless intuit and vocalize melody successfully, and they do so in terms of a movement up and down a pitch space of seamless continuity from low to high, whereas trained musicians invent and perform melody in terms of a highly artificial system of tonal relationships based on aurally discontinuous scales and harmonic series. The gliding tones of ordinary speech tend as melody to settle, like electrons orbiting a nucleus, into stable pitch strata. The 'deep structure' of melody we seek may still emerge as a preference for contour relationships independent of modes and scales, as Parsons's discovery suggests. The question is whether harmonic conventions can be incorporated in a melody synthesis program in a way that does not make the program totally rule-bound.

The distinctive feature of Western melody is an ability to move with equal ease over harmonic intervals of a third or fifth as to an adjacent tone or semitone. Think of the triadic formations in the melody of 'The Beautiful Blue Danube', for example, which in theory should be unsingable, but in practice are not; or the persistent chord formations of Kurt Weill's 'Mack the Knife'. Harmonic shifts of a third or a fifth, not to mention melodic 'faults' that cause a line of melody suddenly to leap to a lower or higher octave, appear to give the lie to the description of melody as a single continuous curve. The opening phrase of 'Blue Danube' draws a curve projected on to widely spaced degrees of a sequence of major triads: D major, A9, A9, D, D, E minor, etc. A tonal melody can thus be subject to 'change-of-state' movement within a chord structure, from tonic to third to fifth to seventh to octave, or convey 'change of direction' transitions linking one chord to the next in a sequence.

Whether a melody interval is perceived as a degree change or as a chord change depends to a large extent on how the listener imagines it to be harmonized. In the absence of explicit harmonization, melody intervals that belong to a common harmony tend to be perceived as degrees of the same chord, whereas those that do not—intervals of a semitone, tone, tritone, or major seventh—are interpreted as corresponding to a change of harmony. The scope for tensions and ambiguities between the two perceptions provides a rich source of expression in tonal music.

Sections of early atonal melody by Arnold Schoenberg, taken from the soprano obbligato (to words by Stefan George) of the third movement of the composer's Op. 10 Second String Quartet, melodies designed moreover to herald a new era of liberation of music from classical tonality, were discovered to correspond to a two-phase cycle consisting of a descending bassline (maximum step interval: 1 tone) to which is added a triadic interval: unison, major third, fifth, or octave. Thus a leap up of a minor third is the product of a bassline decline by one semitone, plus a major third, and a leap of a minor seventh upward the product of a bassline decline by a full tone plus an octave, etc. (Maconie and Cunningham 1978: 209) (Ex. 2). The structure of a melody generated by the Schoenberg program is thus non-symmetrical, since the second-stage tonal interval is always added to the underlying 'drifting tonic', never subtracted from it.

An interesting feature of the Schoenberg program is the apparent ease with which melodies lie within the programmed limits, reflecting a nice equilibrium between drift and added harmonic curves. The program does not require bounce at the lower extreme of range where the drift value is around two semitones (though fractional values are possible). At the upper limit, however, the most musically satisfying results were achieved by a melody about to exceed its upper limit cancelling the added bassline interval of a tone or semitone, while leaving the added harmonic interval intact. This in effect allows a melody to go momentarily beyond its upper limit, but in a wholly plausible way (Ex. 3).

The disagreement dividing Platonist and Aristoxenian theories of melody can be summarized as a difference in priorities. The

Ex. 2. Soprano melody line from Schoenberg, String Quartet No. 2 (1908), 3rd movement (setting of 'Litanei' by Stefan George)

Ex. 3. Fractal melody generated by the Schoenberg 2 program

former theory is concerned above all with exact quantities and ratios, in much the same way as the theory of digital sound depends on a representation of a continuous waveform as a series of discrete voltages. For Aristoxenus, on the other hand, the operative 'analogue' principle is that of continuous motion, with all the implications of range and potential, emotional and otherwise, that that entails. Musical intuition would tend to side with Aristoxenus, but common sense acknowledges the important practical advantages of insisting on standard values for pitch and interval. In the same way that *harmonia* refers not only to music but to orderly relationships in society and the natural world, so we may expect *melos* to comprehend a wider investigation of the laws governing determinism and periodic motion.

Plato's strictures on melody may also be taken as a commentary on the function of vowels and vowel sounds within the Greek language. The Greek alphabet was a hybrid affair, put together around 750 BC from elements of the older Semitic script. This, however, was an alphabet without letters for vowels, in effect translating 'a script for a language in which vocalic differences were relatively insignificant to the Greek language in which they were highly significant' (Olson 1994: 84). Unlike Semitic languages (among whose descendants are modern Arabic and Hebrew), in spoken Greek vowels are unusually charged with meaning. When this feature is added to the fact that vowels are also the natural carriers of speech melody, there is a basis for a science of melody that addresses the musical and expressive dimension of speech. Vocal music in the Western tradition is still vowel orientated: nobody expects the choir to 'sing' the 't-k-t-k' refrains in Messiaen's *Cinq Rechants*. Equally, linguistics is vowel-orientated. In a resonant forum or temple, heightened speech is revealed as vowel-based melody, while consonants dissolve in noise. Plato's strictures against noises and glissandi in melody might just as well reflect a concern to distinguish vowel sounds as stable melodic features of spoken language from consonants and diphthongs that are typically noisy or unstable. His views on *melos* could then be seen as part of a broader discrimination of the features of language that convey sense from those that are responsible for conveying human emotion.

For all their simplicity, the melody programs described above do seem to point to quantifiable differences between melody types, as well as indicating ways of plotting structural resemblances between outwardly very different idioms: after all, the differences between pseudo-Arabic monody and pseudo-Xenakis are only matters of scale. That in itself suggests that not only may Parsons be right in defining melody in terms as basic as changes of direction, but also that rhythmic and tonal conventions may eventually be shown to contribute only cosmetically to the satisfaction communicated by a particular melody.

13

Ratio

Apollo was so potent as a cultural and political symbol that the love-poet Propertius could hang his whole account of Actium around the god's role. It was in Phoebus Apollo's bay that the cosmic struggle took place (*Elegies* 4.6). The enemy fleet was damned in advance by the deified Romulus, Augustus blessed by Jupiter. Apollo leaves Delos to stand above Augustus' prow; he lays aside his lyre and his role as god of music and poetry, and takes up his terrible guise as the avenger of piety and purity, who with his arrows once struck plague into the camp of Agamemnon.

(Wallace-Hadrill 1993: 7)

THE driving force of a bow and arrow is a stretched string. The greater the tension of the string, the greater the pull required and the farther the arrow is able to fly. An archer learns to recognize the characteristics of a stretched string. A long bow has a long string and a long string makes a low-pitched sound of precise pitch: not a noise, a musical note. A smaller bow's shorter string, the tension being the same, will vibrate at a higher pitch. The pitch of a bow-string is not very loud, as the string vibration is heard in isolation from a resonating cavity or container. It is quite distinct enough, nevertheless, to be heard by the archer in control, as the action of drawing a bow brings the hand drawing the string directly past the ear.

String quality is a vital consideration for an archer, and the quality of tone produced by the bowstring is a primary source of information of the quality of manufacture and ongoing condition of a string from day to day. The relationship of bow to string is virtually constant, the bow having been designed to maintain its stiffness and thus the tension of its string throughout its working life. The tone should therefore sound the same in pitch and timbre from one day to the next, though the precise pitch will vary from bow to bow and string to string. Suppose then that a bowstring is heard to change in tone. That would immediately suggest that something was amiss, a lower pitch, for example, indicating a loss of tension arising from wear and tear of bow or string, and a change of timbre or tonal quality suggesting a local deterioration of the string itself. Such checks on string tone are familiar to practising musicians specializing in instruments of the violin, guitar, lute, harp, and similar families. String instruments have the additional capability of being tuned up or down in pitch, which is to say that unlike the longbow, they incorporate mechanisms for raising or lowering the tension of individual strings. They also incorporate resonating boxes or vessels to amplify the sound and make it audible to an audience. Although the stresses imposed on the strings of a musical instrument are far less than on a bowstring, the instrument nevertheless has to be engineered to withstand tensions that, just as for a bow, threaten to warp the support structure out of shape.

Judging the condition of a bowstring at rest is the first and most critical of a series of acoustic tests that accompany the process of loading and shooting an arrow. The tone produced by the freely vibrating string acts as a reference for subsequent tone responses. With insertion of an arrow and as the bow is drawn and released, a further series of tonal cues and checks comes into play.

The point of optimum drive along the length of a bowstring is at its centre. Placing an arrow at the centre makes sense for a number of reasons. The centre is the point of maximum draw, allowing the arrow to achieve optimum flight. The force acting on the arrow at the midpoint is also balanced, to allow it to follow a controlled trajectory.

Placing an arrow at the centre of the bowstring also influences the pitch of the string by interrupting the vibration of the string at that point. Finding the midpoint of a stretched string is the starting-point of the science of musical acoustics, the point at which the fundamental is suppressed and the first harmonic is heard. It is the starting-point of the system of harmonic measures that leads via

Pythagoras and his followers to the modes and scales of Western music, and in a different direction, to the evolution of the slide rule. When an arrow is placed exactly at the midpoint of the string, its full-length vibration is divided into two halves, the pitch sounding an octave higher.

Natural nodes or dead points can be found on a vibrating stretched string such that when it is touched at these points with minimal pressure, e.g. by the point of a quill, the string is prevented from vibrating in some modes but not others. A harpist or violinist can demonstrate this by bowing or plucking an open (unstopped) string and then gently touching it at the midpoint: the vibration continues uninterrupted, but the sounding pitch changes abruptly to the first harmonic, an octave higher. In positioning an arrow, an archer can use a similar technique to find the midpoint of a bowstring, and can do it by listening rather than looking, a vital consideration under battle conditions. Not only does the string tell the archer where the midpoint lies, but also how to stay in place once the midpoint is found, since the pitch of the string with the arrow in position should always be the same above and below the arrow. If the arrow is badly placed, the string vibration is affected, which can be taken as signifying that the arrow is not exactly in place, and therefore cannot be guaranteed to follow a perfect trajectory. When the exact midpoint is found, the string vibrations on either side are in balance and in tune with one another.

[The] early discovery of musical ratios was . . . one of the main starting-points of Greek mathematically orientated science. The discovery meant that an immediately given, subjective, sensible quality was found to be exactly correlated with measurements expressed as simple numerical ratios, all having the same pattern, superparticular (n + 1 : n); and this correlation was established empirically by using the monochord. We feel whether an octave or a fifth is in tune or not, and with great accuracy; we get then exactly in tune, then we measure the strings on our monochord, and lo! they are as 1 : 2; 2 : 3. The whole world of sensible qualities, e.g. hot, cold, dry, wet, might then be explicable in the same way; the ultimate elements, the basic structure of the universe might be found to show similar, though not necessarily identical, simple elegant mathematical ratios. (Walker 1978: 7)

Further aural tests come into play as the arrow is drawn back prior
to release. The action of drawing a bow increases tension on the
string leading to a rise in pitch. In a flawless string the pitches on
either side of the arrow should continue to sound in tune with one
another throughout the rise in pitch. If something gives as the
arrow is drawn, the tuning will deviate from unison, indicating a
local weakness or failure in the bow or its string. The structure and
related process is acoustically monitored in a very simple and efficient manner able to detect flaws and weaknesses otherwise hidden
from the eye, and alert the archer to possible danger. The action of
drawing the bow moves to a release point of maximum tension,
and associated rise of string pitch from a low note associated with
the bowstring in its initial state to a higher and stronger-sounding
note. These low and high reference tones are fixed in the memory
of the operator in the same way that the healthy tone of a motor
cycle or car is fixed in the consciousness of its owner. Animal hearing is structured in such a way that associations can and do form
between constant pitch features in the auditory environment and
localized stimulation of auditory receptors in the inner ear. It means
that a deviation from normal pitch is noticed because the pattern of
receptors excited deviates from normal in a noticeable way.

We can imagine Greek science to have been interested in establishing a formula relating the flight of an arrow to the change of
pitch audible in the bowstring as the arrow is drawn back prior to
release. This change of pitch cannot be explained in simple harmonic terms. The pitch of a string can be changed in two ways:
either by making it longer or shorter, the tension remaining the
same, or by increasing the tension without changing the length. A
monochord is designed to allow both: movable bridges allow the
length to be changed, and adding weights allows the tension to be
affected. By correlating a change of bowstring pitch to a change of
string length on the monochord, a series of linear measures is
obtained for the pitch changes associated with alterations in tension
as the bowstring is drawn back; the same series of pitches can sub-
sequently be correlated to changes in the weighting of a monochord string, to arrive at tension values for a string of unchanging
length. The relationship of length to weight is not as simple as it

may appear. Vincenzo Galilei rebuked his rival Zarlino and, by implication, a number of illustrious predecessors for assuming that the ratios observable between pitches were uniformly the same for the variable forces that produce them.

Galilei gives several examples of Zarlino's lapses . . . One is the case of the ratios of the octave in pipes. Zarlino says they should follow the same rule as strings, namely that a pipe of half the length of another will sound an octave higher than the first. They must be the same width and thickness also, Galilei objects. Zarlino should have experimented (*esperimentato*) first, which would have been very easy to do. Even though Aristotle makes the same mistake, Zarlino, a musician, is not so easily excused. Similarly Plutarch says that weights attached to strings produce an octave when they are in duple proportion. This is false, Galilei maintains, for they have to be in quadruple proportion. (Palisca 1985: 270)

To multiply the frequency of a stretched string by 2 (raise the pitch by one octave) one reduces its sounding length by the reciprocal, ½; to achieve the same doubling of frequency by adding weights, however, a 4 : 1 increase in loading is required. So you end up with a formula that says a change in pitch by a factor x is equivalent to a change in string length (effectively of wavelength) of $1 : (1/x)$, or to a change of tension of $1 : x^2$. The subject is still under debate in the time of Mersenne, one school of thought arguing that the ratio of the octave is two to one, the other that it is four to one ('Traité des instruments', in Crombie 1994: 845). Mersenne believed that the problem had already been solved by the Greeks. Aristotle may be in error, but then Aristotle is not the most reliable guide to Pythagorean science, about which his frequent scepticism may in part be a mask for genuine ignorance. For the Pythagoreans themselves, the question whether they succeeded in reconciling scales of length and force is answered if a convincing formula can in fact be found. This formula would be framed to account for the force exerted on the arrow by the bow in terms relating the change in pitch of the bowstring to the angle subtended by the arrow. The equation can be expressed geometrically, as successive changes of pitch as the bowstring is drawn back can be represented as a series of triangles of which the arrow represents the base, the drawn bowstring the hypotenuse, completed by a vertical

line representing the bowstring at rest. As the length of the base (displacement of the arrow) increases, so the force on the hypotenuse
(the pitch of the bowstring) also increases. The task is to find a simple
conversion formula of linear measure to power (Fig. 5).

(*a*)   (*b*)

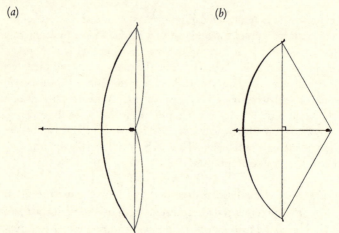

FIG. 5.
(*a*) Bow at rest. The position of the arrow marks the first harmonic.
(*b*) Bow ready for firing. The pressure on the arrow is equivalent to the
force required to change the pitch of the bowstring, whose length
remains constant.

At this point one notices that all such triangles are right-angle triangles. (They are also in pairs, an upper and a lower, which may
explain why right-angle triangles seem always to come in pairs in
the early mathematical literature.) And we arrive at a formula
which says that the tension on the string is equal to the square on
the hypotenuse, which is equal to the sum of the squares on the
other two sides. So Pythagoras' theorem, which we learned at
school as a purely geometrical curiosity with applications in sur-
veying, may have been arrived at as a simple formula for calculat-
ing the relative force propelling an arrow from a bow, based on the
acoustics of the bowstring. When the formula was discovered, it is
said there was great celebration among the Pythagoreans. The
example of the bow provides a model for the Platonic concept of

temperament and of modes as expressions of human character and fortitude. Drawing a connection between the art of music and the art of archery likewise establishes a link between the emotions aroused by music, the tuning of the lyre, and the sound of a bow being drawn. Hence Apollo's prowess with the bow as well as the lyre; hence too the association of erotic tension with Cupid's arrows, and desire with the plucking of heartstrings.

A similar motivation is able to account for the attention devoted by the Pythagorean school to the right-angle triangle of sides 1 : 1 and hypotenuse the square root of 2. A triangle of equal sides can be construed, in the context of experimenting with a bowstring, as an attempt to reconcile tension and length starting from an initial assumption of equality between the two. The bowstring at rest can be regarded as a triangle of which the sides are 1 and zero, and the hypotenuse is also 1. A triangle of sides 1 : 1 by comparison imposes an additional tension on the string equivalent to doubling the original length, and the expectation is a linear value for the hypotenuse that bears some relationship to the octave ratio implied by the linear displacement. Finding that the result corresponds to an irrational number would lead to a search for values that were not irrational, logically by permutations of whole-number ratios. After 1 : 1, they would try 2 : 1, then 3 : 2, and 4 : 3, at which point the length of the hypotenuse is miraculously revealed, not only as 5, a real number, but one furthermore that is acoustically in harmony [3, 4, 5] with the other two sides.

The square root of 2, on the other hand, is not abandoned; it remains as a thorn in the side of universal harmony, and survives as the irrational number determining a rational division of the octave into equal-tempered intervals. Though both scales are Pythagorean inventions, it is important to distinguish the equal-tempered scale (as favoured in modern keyboard tuning) from the traditional Pythagorean temperament based on rational numbers corresponding to harmonic intervals. Equal temperament we can regard as a mathematical solution to the bowstring problem; Pythagorean temperament is a separate musical derivative of the mathematical scale. 'With the discovery of irrational quantities, also attributed to the Pythagoreans, come other probable cases of musical influence on mathematics, such as the early invention of methods of succes-sive approximation to the square root of 2 or other surds' (Walker 1978: 7).

The famous paradox attributed to Zeno the Pythagorean also addresses the relationship between pitch and linear measure. It has come down to us as a logical puzzle, but it gains additional depth if we imagine it as being told with the aid of a monochord. Ostensibly it is a story of Achilles, or the hare (i.e. a natural athlete) in a race with a tortoise (a natural slowcoach) along a defined course to a common finishing-point. Achilles can run twice as fast as the tortoise, and gives the tortoise a half-way start. In theory, he should catch up with the tortoise on the finishing line; in practice, he can never make it (Fig. 6).

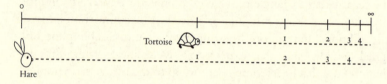

FIG. 6.   Zeno's Paradox. Achilles is represented by the hare.

Note: The 'course' to be run is the pitch space of a monochord (stretched string). The tortoise maintains his octave lead despite being only half as fast as the hare. The string length is finite, but the distance to be covered in pitch terms is infinite.

If we imagine the string of the monochord as the length of the course (a guitar or lute string is still called a *course* today, inciden-tally), Achilles starts at the end, the tortoise at the half-way point—an octave higher. Achilles races up the first octave: do re mi fa so la ti do. But the tortoise has covered half the remaining distance, and this is the point: he is still a whole octave ahead. Achilles catches up another octave, and the tortoise is now in front by half the remaining length of the course, and is still an octave ahead. In the acoustic version of the story, no matter how close Achilles gets to the tortoise in linear terms, the tortoise is always the same dis-tance ahead in pitch terms as it was at the outset. So Achilles can never catch up, and since the distance to be covered in pitch terms is infinite, the race itself never ends. Zeno's fable is thus an illustration of the paradoxical relationship between linear measure, representing visual reality, and pitch measure, representing acoustic reality. The message it conveys is that the world of acoustics is not commensurate with the real world; indeed, it implies the existence of an irrational or superior acoustical universe in parallel with the universe of visual perception.

Other echoes of Pythagorean mysteries survive in folklore. There are a number of clues, for example, in the nursery tale of Jack and the Beanstalk, and they emerge quite naturally when the story is told to the accompaniment of a stringed instrument such as a fiddle, lute, or guitar. A 'jack' is a term for a plectrum; the story action describes movement up a stalk (an ascending scale up the fingerboard) to a world above the clouds, i.e. a world of harmonics; it involves a giant or ogre who likes to eat small boys (an image of the fundamental tone 'consuming' the higher octave harmonic); and it involves a 'singing harp', an image of acoustic practices relating voice formants to harmonics. The deciding factor, however, is the ogre's magic incantation 'Fee, fie, foh, fum!', which is certainly not meaningless in acoustics, but is a mnemonic for singing and monitoring vowels as sympathetically vibrating harmonics of accompanying string tone. If the four syllables are sung carefully to an accompanying tone of constant pitch, the voice formants associated with the changing vowels will be heard as ringing harmonics in descending sequence. For instance, harmonics 16, 8, 6, and 3 over a sung fundamental C3 (C below middle C).

Another Jack appears in the nursery rhyme 'Jack and Jill'. This is interesting because the traditional melody to the rhyme consists largely of harmonics, suggesting that it may have been sung to the accompaniment of a tromba marina, which despite its name is a bowed monochord (Ex. 4). In the key of C, the melody starts on harmonic 6 (G), moving in succession to harmonics 8 (C), 9 (D), 10 (E), and back to 8 (C); begins again at 6 (G), rises to 7 (B flat), falling back to 6 (G), 5 (E), and ending on 4 (low C). The voice line, however, does not follow the harmonics exactly. Where the instrument plays harmonic 7, B flat, the voice wants to sing A, a semitone lower; but the instrument can't play A, so a dissonance is created, coinciding neatly with the two points in the verse that refer to pain ('*broke* his crown' and '*mend* his head'). Passing notes are inserted in the last phrase to emphasize the downward movement G–(F)–E–(D)–C 'Jill came tumbling after'.

Ex. 4.   'Jack and Jill'

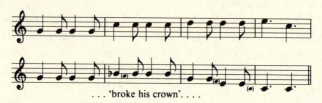

. . . 'broke his crown'. . . .

harmonics on C-tuned tromba marina

∟ dissonant 7th

14

Instruments

ALL musical instruments are transducers. A transducer is a device that converts one kind of energy, the physical input of a performer, into another form of energy, which is radiated chiefly as sound. In a musical context what is normally of primary interest to a listener is the quality and beauty of instrumental tone, in itself and in relation to the music composed for it; appreciation of performing artistry follows close after that. A listener can give due consideration to an expert performance given artistic terms of reference, and these are embodied in the structure and techniques required of a musical instrument, and in the musical information to be conveyed.

Every musical instrument, however, has another agenda. Sometimes the other agenda is self-evident: for example, that trumpets make good signalling instruments, and that drums are good for reinforcing a beat. That is also how these instruments are conventionally portrayed in the music we hear. For other instruments the underlying implications of a particular structure or timbre are less obvious. What is the purpose of an oboe, for instance? Why is the front of a lute flat, and the back curved, whereas front and back of a violin are both curved? Do such features have any other purpose than their contribution to a particular musical instrument? If an instrument has no obvious function other than to make musical noises, then one begins to ask how, or rather why it evolved in the first place.

Musical instruments are played and controlled in different ways. Strings are plucked, bowed, or hammered; wind instruments are played by pressurized air; percussion instruments are struck with a variety of beaters. These various modes of excitation group down into two major categories: instantaneous, as for plucking and percussion instruments, and continuous, as for bowed, and wind instruments, and electric keyboards. The different implications of instantaneous and continuous modes of excitation are highly significant. For example, they imply different concepts and experiences of time. A plucked or percussion instrument is required to give an instant response to an immediate action: in acoustic terms, all the information inherent in the instrument and specific to a given mode of excitation (plectrum, stick, hammer, etc.) has to be initiated at the same moment, the time of attack. What happens after the action of plucking or striking is largely due to the manner in which the excess energy is dissipated through the system, which is down to how the instrument is engineered: the distribution of forces in a piano, for example, involves the same engineering principles as for a suspension bridge. Though musicians are always looking for ways of extending the expressive range of their instruments, using vibrato to influence a guitar note after the string is plucked, or the pedals to modify the evolution of piano tone, the essential character of a plucked or percussion instrument consists in the manner of its natural response, as a closed system of vibrating members and resonators, to a particular action at a moment in time. That response, the richness of sound and smoothness or complexity of its evolution and decay, tells a listener about the behaviour of wood, metal, and skin products, whether they are strings, struts, or surfaces, and about their shapes, their size, and their efficiency in converting input energy into sound.

For bowed strings and wind instruments (including the voice) very different transduction processes obtain. With these instruments the input of energy may be either abrupt and virtually instantaneous (staccato), or gradual and controlled (legato), and the instrument has to be able to respond with appropriate speed, not only rapidly for staccato, but also with a more gradual rise to a steady state vibration for a legato attack. Since tone continuation for these instruments depends on a continuous input of bow friction or air pressure from the player, the coupled system consists of the player and the instrument in active partnership, and is not simply a passive resonating system characterized by the relationship of parts within the instrument alone.

Control over the evolution of a musical tone places a responsibility on the performer to maintain a steady signal. The duration of a violin tone is limited by the length of the bow, speed of bowing, skill in changing bow direction, and evenness of bow pressure, and of a wind tone by the length of a breath, and pace and evenness of breath release. The dependence of tone continuation on performer action means that where the input of energy falters, continuity of tone will also falter. Inasmuch as consistency of tone is musically required or perceptually expected, deviations will be perceived as a consequence of human error. Human error is not exposed in this way among plucked and percussion instruments; the up side of one's technique being so exposed, however, is the option of deliberately exploiting inconsistencies of tone for expressive effect. With some instruments the possibilities of expressive modulation of tone are greater than others: with trumpets the possibilities are limited, for saxophones they are richer, and for violins and cellos they are positively vast.

Certain instruments incorporate mechanical sustain. A harmonium bellows is sustained at pressure by pedal action; instruments of the bagpipe family employ a bladder as an air reservoir independent of the lungs and enabling indefinite sustain. The hurdy-gurdy incorporates a manually rotated disc friction mechanism as an alternative to the bow to keep the strings vibrating; modern organs and synthesizers rely on electric power. Although these instruments are capable of indefinite sustain, their sustain is curiously lacking in expression for want of direct 'tension' (the Greek word is useful here) between player and instrument. For plucked string and percussion instruments, the essentially alien demands of evolutionary and expressive sustain have to be satisfied by rapidly reiterated attacks: the chord strumming of a Spanish guitar, the shake on one note of a mandolin, a piano trill, a harp bisbigliando alternation of enharmonic tones, a drum roll, a xylophone tremolo, and so on. Similar effects can also be produced on bowed string instruments by tremolo (the 'bumble-bee' effect) and on winds by 'flutter-tongue' or throat tremolo (the rolled 'rrr'). Repetitive sustain creates sounds of richer and noisier texture than continuous sustain, but is a much less efficient use of performer energy.

Gongs and bells are a special group of percussion instruments designed to make sounds that not only compel but are also able to sustain the listener's attention by creating a sound that is constantly in a process of evolution rather than simply fading away. We can learn something of the culture from the nature and complexity of each instrument's qualities of tone and reverberation. They were designed to convey a technological and a political message, of a technical ability to cast and work metal on a large scale, and to create alloys of a purity and quality that could be readily heard in the grandeur and consistent power of the sounds produced by these marvels of science and industry. That certain societies express themselves in the sound of bells and gongs that are designed to resonate at specific pitches, while other societies are represented by instruments of indefinite pitch such as tam-tams and cymbals, also tells us something about underlying cultural and intellectual priorities. The implicit message of European bell design is that a structure engineered to resonate at specific frequencies—in the sense also that a society may be imagined to function as a vibrating system—is more efficient in the way it processes energy, and its sound is also more enduring as a result. So the inner life of the bell sound corresponds to the inner life of a particular organization of society. A large tam-tam, on the other hand, is a model of power distribution that starts at the centre and feeds out to the edges, without the positive feedback and coherent partial structure of the bell. Acoustically, however, the tam-tam conveys an impression of sunlike brilliance and radiance, of a dazzling and overwhelming richness of effect. The bell, by contrast, sounds more like a civil servant than a *roi soleil*: an image of delegated rather than absolutely centralized power.

As the operative principles of string instruments have to do with tension and resonance, so those of wind instruments have to do with pressure waves and energy flows. The wind moans. Its sound rises and falls in pitch, like the wordless keening of someone in pain. The rise and fall in pitch is a reflection of an air current varying in speed, and variation in speed can be produced not only by atmospheric conditions, but also by the wind encountering an obstacle or conduit, natural or man-made, in its path that has the effect of making it audible as a movement in pitch. When we face headlong into the full blast of a gale in the open air, the sound that assaults our ears is a noise filling the range of audible frequencies from low to high. Any conversion of the inherent noisiness of wind motion into audible tone, even when it is a tone of fluctuating and inconstant pitch, signifies that the random motion has had a structure imposed on it by some means, to create a waveform or regular oscillation of pressure at audible frequency. Usually when the wind is heard to moan, it sounds in the range of a female voice, signifying a frequency range in the region of 200–500 hertz. Hence the sexist association of the wailing wind with the female of the species.

The moaning of the wind and the controlled pitches of wind instruments of music are both effects of a movement of air in a confined space being forced into regular vibration. In order to harness the wind, one has to control its speed and direction of flow, and also the friction of surfaces by which the flow is directed. To ensure a unidirectional flow of air, the fipple flute or recorder incorporates a wedge-shaped obstruction within the airway that has the effect of creating a pressure difference to draw the air current in one direction. The Elizabethan heyday of recorder craft coincided with advances in chimney design and construction that employ a similar principle to prevent smoke and soot from blowing back.

The lip-reed interface between player and instrument is a valve; the art of playing a wind instrument is an art of controlling the relationship between air pressure and a release mechanism, in the case of woodwinds a single reed or double reed that is forced open to admit a pressure pulse into the air column, and in the case of brass instruments the role played by the player's pursed lips inside a cup or tapered mouthpiece. For woodwind instruments the player's mouth is clamped around the reed, making an airtight seal, the lips themselves being relatively unstressed; for brass instruments the airtight seal is produced by pressure pushing the lips outward against the mouthpiece: this is hard on the lips and requires careful rationing of effort and playing time, not to mention a regular supply of beer.

For a single- or double-reed wind instrument to 'speak' or produce a controllable musical tone, the relationship of air pressure and reed mechanism has to be precisely matched. At a critical point the valve opens, releasing a pulse of air into the air column. Pressure within the mouth cavity immediately drops, and the valve closes, allowing more pressure to build up, and the process repeats. Introducing a pressure front into the air column institutes an equalization process in which the pressure front expands away from the mouthpiece end, contained and in some cases helped along by a gradually widening inner bore. When the pressure front encounters an open finger hole, or reaches the bell, it passes into the open air, causing pressure within the air column to drop. This low-pressure zone travels back up the tube to the mouthpiece like air travelling back up a test tube when its contents are poured away. A push–pull cycle of pressure and release rapidly builds up on either side of the reed valve, regulating the escape of pressure pulses to a constant frequency. That frequency of pulse release is governed by the distance the pressure pulse travels down the tube to the point where it can escape. If it only has to go a short distance, the lapse of time before the pressure drops and a new pulse is admitted is relatively brief; if it has to travel twice the distance to reach a finger hole, the drop in pressure takes twice as long to return. Since a musical tone consists of regular fluctuations in air pressure, the frequency at which these fluctuations zigzag back and forth determines the pitch that we hear, and as the distance of travel governs the timing of pressure changes, the position of the first open finger hole along the airway determines the wavelength and thereby the pitch.

Airway design in musical instruments provides a foundation of knowledge for the development of systems and controls for the regulation of fluid flow from early irrigation systems and domestic watercourses to the modern internal combustion engine and ramjet. The rapid proliferation of new brass instruments and brass band activity in nineteenth-century Western Europe coincided with equivalent advances in civil engineering, most notably in the construction of town water and sewage systems. The development of punched-card control mechanisms for industrial weaving and calculation coincided with the development of the steam-powered fairground calliope and pedal-operated player piano, both of which play from punched paper tape.

Why the organ was invented is something of a mystery. Even the best authorities give an impression of the organ having arrived fully formed in the sixteenth century, just in time to take advantage of baroque polyphony. This convenient assumption does not alas explain a period of gestation and development stretching over some 2,000 years. Such dedication may have led to J. S. Bach and the wonders of the 'Vom Himmel Hoch' variations, but were certainly not the reason for embarking on the journey in the first place.

What can have been the initial motivation for embarking on a project that was destined to preoccupy science and engineering for thousands of years? First, to explain timbre: why sounds of distinctly different tone quality were nevertheless able to come together in unison and to interact, as a voice can excite sympathetic vibrations selectively in a register of freely vibrating strings of graded sizes. Second, the study of materials, in accounting for the nature of resonance, from observations that resonators made of wood, ceramic, bone, various metals, etc. are all able to resonate to the same initiating sound signal, but do so in ways revealing of their different acoustic properties. Third, the study of communication, in particular the nature of vowels, since a voice is not only an individual timbre or tone of voice in respect of its structure as a resonator, but is a source of modulated timbre as an instrument of language. Understanding timbre promised more than accounting for the differences between the voice and the lyre as vibrating structures: it was the key to isolating the features of a singing voice signal—vowel timbres—that convey intelligence.

Why experiment with pipes and not with strings? Stretched strings over a resonating frame form a lightweight and responsive instrument for investigating and isolating the distinctive peak resonances of vowel tone, making instruments such as the Aeolian harp, harps, and psalteries likely sources of early knowledge of the composite nature of speech sounds as harmonics in various combinations and intensities. The advantages of string mechanisms—sensitive, tunable, portable—become disadvantages when interest turns from analysis to synthesis of tones of different timbre. For synthesis, reliability is the primary concern, meaning consistency of tone and stability of pitch, and this cannot be guaranteed with lightweight structures involving strings that can change their tuning with changes in atmospheric temperature and humidity. Pipes have the advantages of being made of more inert substances and of maintaining their pitch. In place of a bank of tuned strings, therefore, came the development of an instrument based on pan-pipes, but at lower frequencies and on a much larger scale.

Wind instruments rely on wind power, and wind power in the shape of a human player is not always able to deliver the same pressure to more than one pipe at a time. The development of a pipe synthesizer therefore had to involve some form of artificial regulator of wind pressure to ensure that a given combination of pipes received a flow of air at precisely the same pressure. The *hydraulis* or water organ is evidence of an application to acoustics of principles of fluid mechanics investigated in depth by Archimedes, Philo of Alexandria, and others. Naturally control of air pressure by water pressure (hydrostatics) has significant implications in other fields. There were many other applications to be considered. Musical acoustics remained an issue, however, as a means of verifying and monitoring the behaviour of water-powered devices intended for other purposes: we recognize these in the domestic pressure cooker that whistles to signal that the water has boiled, and the ritual train whistle that tells passengers that the boiler is up to steam and the engine is ready to go.

Musical automata are among the achievements of Islamic scientists of the Middle Ages who absorbed and developed many of the discoveries of their Greek antecedents. 'These are often simple, single-note devices, such as the mechanical whistle used to simulate the sound of the trumpet in al-Jazari's first clock. He does, however, describe several machines specifically designed as musical automata, although he is more concerned with describing the production of a flow of air for operating the instruments than with the instruments themselves; indeed, the latter are hardly described at all' (Hill 1993: 143). Donald Hill also mentions an account of a remarkable mechanical flute dating from the tenth century AD, a nine-hole instrument operated by a keyboard controlled by levers engaging teeth on a rotating cylinder, a device more sophisticated in engineering terms than the mechanical organ described by Athanasius Kircher in 1650 (Hill 1993: 145).

The organ's massive size, from what we know of the earliest European instruments, demands a commensurate largeness of scale of the environment acting as resonator for experiments in the acoustics of tone combination. Large pipes and low frequencies mean wavelengths of a size that can only be accommodated in buildings of great size, indeed of superhuman scale, a reason for the growth in size of churches and cathedrals at the end of the millennium, a change of scale beyond the plausible requirements of population growth or propitiation of divine power. Gothic cathedrals in their day were temples of acoustic science, and the case for ever larger cathedrals was the same as for ever larger particle accelerators in the twentieth century: the bigger the scale, the larger the wave structure that can be studied, and the greater the detail of the wave structure of the universe that can thereby be revealed. And the old organs also consumed vast amounts of energy to achieve very modest results, just like today's particle accelerators. Instruments so obviously unsuited for musical performance as we understand it can only have been devised for some other purpose, and acoustical experimentation is the only logical purpose for these extraordinary devices. Why go to all that trouble merely to provide the officiating cantor or choir with a starting note?

We know that the control interface problem was solved by the fifteenth century because instruments of that era survive. The great craftsmen who succeeded in miniaturizing organ keyboards and servo-mechanisms for controlling pitch and registration made it possible for composers and music to develop rapidly in entirely new directions, combining multiple voices in intricate musical structures. Just as all this creative energy was reaching a peak the church authorities began to express doubts about the use and abuse of music in a religious environment. Responsibility for authorizing music passed from the priestly class to the musicians, its servants. The locus of musical activity shifted from the cathedral to the basilica, and from the basilica to the palace, symbolically abandoning the centralized power structure of the great organ in favour of orchestras, self-governing collectives of mixed players. The concept of symphony survived, but as human organization and activity. In that context of social modelling, the role of classical music also became more orientated to human needs and pleasures, and forgot about its scientific origins.

The acoustics of instruments and architecture also coincide in the world of baroque and classical music. The violin's complex curves make it an efficient resonator in all directions, unlike the lute, for example, which is shaped like an automobile headlamp and produces a focused directional beam of sound. The violin family's combination of robust construction, brilliance of tone, and omnidirectionality allow these instruments to function successfully in surroundings less reverberant than the church, and also to function as instrumental choirs, producing a diffuse, radiant tone. In addition to propagating sound relatively equally in all directions, the violin family of instruments by virtue of their curved construction are unusually efficient resonators at any pitch, not having the preference for certain keys that we associate with the guitar, baroque flute, or the diatonic keyboard. That combination of features makes the violin an especially suitable medium for a new Renaissance humanist aesthetic of emotional expression, and for musical experimenting in freely varying key relationships.

The violin provided the basis for the new baroque orchestra, an ensemble of players interpreting complex written musical procedures. The Italian repertoire of the early baroque era is a wonderful burgeoning of instrumental writing to discover the characters and potentials of newly invented and modified instruments, many of them designed to allow players greater freedom of expression. Loss of the windcap was a comparable development in woodwind instruments. Whereas the shawm, a double-reed instrument, has an enclosed mouthpiece or windcap in order to stabilize the player's breath at a relatively steady pressure, by the time the shawm takes its place as the oboe in the baroque orchestra, it no longer has a windcap, and the player's lips being in direct contact with the reeds are therefore able to influence much more closely the inflection and expression of a melodic line. Baroque music invokes a new sense of individual dynamism and uncertainty, of tone production as well as of tonal development. The musical aesthetic of the baroque age is one of restless transition from one key centre to another, expressed in the familiar moving basslines of Pachelbel and Bach. A music of constant change of harmonic reference is accommodated in baroque architecture, whose curved surfaces and disturbed symmetries are acoustically adapted to varying harmonies. We therefore discern a connection, based on the acoustic properties of curved resonators, between the origins of the violin family and the spatial rhetoric of the great baroque palaces.

There is a wonderful ending to the song cycle *Epitaph for García Lorca* by George Crumb where the soprano solo leans under the wing of the grand piano like a lonely driver peering into the open bonnet of a disabled automobile, and her final tones of lament are resonated in ghostly fashion by the piano strings (an effect incidentally intended to convey an impression of echoing emptiness). In such gestures we remember the Greeks, and their discovery that string instruments such as the harp and the lyre were employed as a means of tuning the singing voice, but in addition to reinforcing the fundamental tone of a singing voice, the strings of a harp were also known to vibrate sympathetically to prominent voice overtones of higher pitch, and that these voice overtones varied from vowel to vowel. The attraction of modelling combinations of harmonically related tones to produce synthetic timbres can be imagined as leading to an acoustic grand unified theory capable of accounting for the variety of animal, vegetable and mineral nature as Heraclitean variations on a limited repertoire of vibratory states.

15

Death and Transfiguration

> And [Samson] turned aside to see the carcase of the lion: and,
> behold, there was a swarm of bees and honey in the carcase
> of the lion . . . Out of the strong came forth sweetness.
>
> (Judges 14: 8, 14)

SAMSON was in no mood to be intimidated by the lion's roar. He
had only just caught sight of the woman of Timnath, and his hor-
mones made him fearless. In the fight that followed he wrestled
with the lion and broke its neck. Later, passing by the same place
on the way to meeting the family of the object of his affections, he
was distracted by a sound of buzzing at the scene of the earlier
encounter, and investigating discovered a hive of bees in residence
in the body cavity of the dead animal. The Old Testament image is
good advertising but dubious science. It remains a potent example
of the persuasiveness of advertising. The MGM lion's roar at the
start of a feature movie is communicating much the same message
of elemental power rendered harmless as benign family entertainment. But while as a symbol of regeneration it continues to work
effectively, as an image of life on the land it is simply untrue: bees
do not colonize the empty ribcage of a dead lion.

Virgil brings a more practised observation to bear in relation to
bees and their origins:

> In hollow cork-trees bees are wont to swarm
> Or in the rotten belly of an oak
>
> (*Georgics II*)

His is perhaps the impatient riposte of a rural poet to old-fashioned
superstition. It is a true observation, but to the question whether it
conveys the same message, the answer is a qualified perhaps not. An

oak does not symbolize the same kind of strength as a lion, nor does the tree have to die in order to provide a hollow in which bees may live, reproduce, and store food. Something about the old, unscientific image tells us that the lion, and more important, the lion being dead, is part of the point of the metaphor: there is a symmetry between the image of a dynamic force of nature ending and a new dynamism beginning, a symmetry that is lost if the lion, once master of the plains, now an empty shell, is replaced by a tree symbolizing a strength that nevertheless endures. We are dealing with an image of death and resurrection, or death and transfiguration. What was once the king of beasts, embodiment of order in the wild, authority, strength, and action, becomes the habitation of a society of bees, and thus a source of honey. 'Out of strength comes forth sweetness.'

Modern (that is, post-classical) opinion has a simple and cynical explanation. Samson's riddle is an example of poetic licence. It is not true and was not meant to be true. With hindsight we realize that what were reported to be bees swarming around the desiccated remains of a slain wild animal can only have been carrion flies feeding on the corpse; that sweetness hanging in the air was the scent of decay and not that of nectar. We know better now, and the message of the scriptures is worthy in other ways. And from our superior wisdom we make excuses. Real science is arguably out of place in a context of myth and morality. That the image of bees spontaneously generated from the body of a lion is literally untrue does not mean that the message it conveys about death and transfiguration—a philosophical argument impacting directly on the attitudes and beliefs of ordinary citizens—is necessarily compromised. Religion is meant to strain credulity.

Needless to say, a literal reading of the text and rationalization of its central error has the effect of diverting a reader's attention from other possible layers of meaning. The lion and bees are also symbolic of forms of society and government. The poet may also be saying that the strength and ruthlessness of a natural order ruled by force is destined to give way to a superior system of social organization in which every member works in co-operation to ensure the survival and prosperity of society as a whole. The sweetness arising from such a system of collective self-regulation can be understood as an expression of energy that would otherwise be directed toward combat and defence, being released into production of the finer things of life, things that make life enjoyable and sustain public morale. Such a reading can be understood to have political undertones, as a warning to dictators and discreet encouragement to proponents of alternative and more democratic systems of government.

But even the political metaphor doesn't quite jell either. For it to work, even as poetry, there has to be a plausible connection between the dead lion image and the swarm of bees image, and so far the image doesn't stand the test either of factual accuracy or of biological necessity. An image of flies buzzing round a corpse is real, though distasteful, and there is a real, if distasteful, connection between the death of the animal and the nourishment of a new generation of flies. But flies are not an ordered society, and they produce no honey, only nuisance value and disease. It is difficult to imagine an author even in those times believing his readers would be taken in by the pretence that flies were as disciplined and productive a society as bees. Perhaps this Dali-esque image is intentionally ambiguous to protect the poet from the literal-minded censors of the day, by allowing them an 'educated' interpretation of democracy (the society of bees) as merely a fanciful illusion (the reality being flies) put about to impress an uneducated lower class, and its so-called sweetness not honey at all, but merely a distasteful consequence of the corruption of the strong and great.

Implausible. Everybody knows that bees gather nectar and pollen from flowers and that nectar is made into honey and pollen is made into honeycomb. Only the most gullible listener is going to be persuaded into imagining that the body cavity of the lion is anything more than a convenient empty container for bees to take refuge, a role that might just as well be assumed by a hollow oak as a dead animal, or if animal an ox, elephant, or humble antelope, since there is no necessary connection between the lion (as a source of strength) and the honey (as a source of sweetness). The image 'out of strength comes forth sweetness' dissolves away into a sleight of phrase, 'out of' as a banal 'emerging from' when you initially thought it to mean 'a product of', or 'created by'.

In their preoccupation with literal truth, post-classical readers miss the aural connection. They forget that verse was written to be listened to rather than read, and that the context of an aural culture is the language of sounds. The image of a dead lion transformed into living bees makes perfect musical sense, and is capable of being understood as an acoustic image expressed in material terms, particularly among cultures where poetry is recited to the accompaniment of a musical instrument. Remember that the classic lyre and its close relation the kithara are forms of stringed instrument actually modelled on the head of a horned animal such as an ox or deer, the skull providing a resonator and the horns a frame for the strings. In playing a lyre a musician was understood to be creating sweet music with the empty vocal chamber of a wild animal, using strings made from its dried and tautened sinews. Animal parts were regularly recycled into music in ancient times: the jawbone of an ass as a ratchet, legbones fashioned into flutes, the skin on its back reconstituted as the resonant surface of a drum. 'The two principal meanings of the term *vox*—a meaningful sound produced by an ensouled being and a pitch—may not have been conceptually so different as they appear to be to us now. The pitchless sounds of nature—such as the splashing of water, the creaking of doors and the crackle of flames—are rarely mentioned in philosophical discussions on sound. The roar of the bull is discussed in the pseudo-Aristotelian *Problemata* only because it is high-pitched and explicable in terms of stretched tendons in the bull's abdomen' (Burnett 1991: 47).

We can go even further. There is coincidentally a real musical instrument surviving from ancient times called the 'lion's roar', and it can be heard showing its paces in the twentieth-century music of Edgar Varèse (*Amériques*, *Hyperprism*, and *Ionisation*). It consists of a barrel-shaped single-headed drum out of the centre of which extends a length of cord, in effect a 'vocal cord' of heavy-duty gut string, passing through a hole in the centre of the skin and secured by a knot. The instrument is played by the player pulling upward on the string with a resin-powdered leather, its friction transmitting a continuous vibration of growling pitch down the cord to the drum skin. The intensity of the growl varies with the amount of friction, and the pitch rises and falls with the tension of the drum skin as it is pulled. The resulting sound is a formidable roar calculated to impress a listener as an image of living (or, for a 1990s audience, dinosaur) power. (A toy version surviving in Germany under the name *Waldteufel* employs a length of cobbler's twine attached to the parchment membrane of a paper cup. It makes the sound of a clucking chicken.)

For a preliterate audience the musical point of the poet's analogy is obvious. As the words are sung, the instrument is plucked, giving audible point to the idea of civilized music emerging from the dessicated remains of the king of beasts. The idea of a lion's sinews being made into the strings of a poet's lyre might be fanciful, but is hardly outrageous. But that still leaves the other half of the equation, the sound of the bees, to be accounted for. Audiences are clearly being asked to make something more than just the connection between the idea of brute force implied by a lion's roar and the idea of sweetness embodied in the sound of a lyre. There has to be a 'bee' element in the equation, and furthermore one connecting bees, through their sound, with music. The answer has to lie in the humming of bees.

By a happy coincidence, the sound of bees is also best imitated by bowed or plucked strings vibrating freely. When Rimsky-Korsakov came to compose *Flight of the Bumble-bee* he chose the bowed string timbre of a violin. A violin is an instrument whose sound is created by friction applied to stretched strings of gut attached to a curved hollow resonator strengthened internally by ribs. Played tremolando, with rapid back-and-forth action on the string, it makes a convincing buzz. So here is a connection, based on the vibration of a stretched string, between the sound of bees and the sound of a lion roaring.

There's only one problem. Bees, even the solitary bumble-bee, don't make the kind of melody Rimsky-Korsakov composed. It is a delightful piece of music, but not an image of bees. Bees tend to hum at a constant pitch, their sound being produced by their wings vibrating at a constant rate. When bees take off, the humming is switched on, so to speak, and when they settle on a flower, the humming abruptly stops. It doesn't slow down with a downward curve in pitch, it doesn't accelerate to take off with a rising curve in pitch. A piece of music based on the actual flight pattern of a bee would strike a listener as intermittent and monotonous, and much less amusing and interesting than the portrait in sound Rimsky has actually composed. A more likely source of the composer's inspiration, in an uncanny echo of the scriptural metaphor, turns out to be the musically more interesting flight pattern of a bluebottle, whose familiarly obsessive and erratic motions are expressed in melodic images that zoom and power dive unsteadily in a melody that buzzes tirelessly around a note and then darts away to a related key. But Rimsky could hardly have made a popular concert encore item out of a composition called *Flight of the Bluebottle* (even though his friend Mussorgsky had a hit with his 'Song of the Flea', which has a refrain based on a musical image of hopping and scratching). Added to which, a bumble-bee has a more friendly public image than a bluebottle or blowfly. So *Flight of the Bumble-bee* it is.

Compared to a lion's roar, which conveys an impression of solitary power in short-lived glissando bursts of intense noise, the more subdued humming of bees presents an image of sustained, purposeful activity in tones of close to uniform pitch. A bee's buzzing does not 'bend' like a bluebottle's, which changes in pitch as it changes in direction and speed, though the sound of a bee actively foraging does acquire a degree of rhythmic accentuation. But the analogy of bees with music is not after all a melodic analogy. The allusion refers to the musical nature of the sound, not to a particular sequence or pattern of notes. It is enough that the sound of buzzing bees can be suggested by the buzz of a string vibrating, whether it be a bowstring being tested for tension, the whizz of a slingshot, or the gentler whirr of wind through rigging. The music of bees is the music of constancy of pitch, which far from being boring to classical listeners lacking the benefit of a recorded music culture, expressed the acoustic virtues of persistence, fortitude, steadiness, and control: virtues of a kind recognizable today in the serene murmur of a well-tuned motor.

The impression of power conveyed by a lion's roar is at the same time an image of dissipation, of energy wasted. By comparison, the continuous buzz of bees and sustained tone of a plucked or bowed string represent correspondingly more efficient systems of energy generation and conservation. In acoustic terms, a transformation of lion into bees makes the point that power concentrated in a single individual is ultimately less efficient than the same amount of power distributed in small amounts among a multitude. Finally the energy of a lion, expressed in largely destructive acts of leadership, is contrasted with the energy that bees make available as food in honey, to restore the strength and delight the taste. A complex and many-layered image leads through the conservation of acoustic energy back to the original starting-point of strength and leadership, but it is a strength transformed and restored in the image of industrious legions starting the day on a honey cake.

Death and resurrection myth is about the persistence of life (continuity of energy) in successive forms. Today the talk is of renewable and recycled energy where two thousand and more years ago the simpler message was 'you are what you eat'. Energy manifests itself in life and life is sustained by means of energy transactions: the consumption of food, which is stored energy; defence, which is self-preservation; the organization of labour, which is management of energy resources; and the imposition of social and moral laws and modes of communication aimed at preventing internal friction and loss of energy affecting the performance of society as a whole. In all of these determinations of classical philosophy musical imagery has a clarifying role to play. But music has another side, as a medium of expression. The talismanic function of musical acoustics imagery is complemented and also subverted by music acting as an outlet of individual emotion which by definition expresses the reverse of self-control and socially productive activity. Loving, suffering, drunken humanity expresses itself in song. The classical message of death and resurrection embodied in the image of bees created out of the body of a lion expresses a classically dispassionate attitude to mortality. People die, life goes on. The death of the lion allows an arguably more organized form of life to arise. Through the destructive brutalities of war human society is enabled to survive. In all of this the idea of music as an expression of individual emotion does not enter the equation; the death of the lion is reconciled as a simple fact with the correspondingly orderly values of Pythagorean musical science. Virgil's imagery of a coexistence of oak tree and bees is if anything even less burdened by moral or emotional overtones.

The Greek theologians were not primarily concerned with the death of Christ; they were concerned with life, and the death was so to speak a mere incident in the life. Their view of the atonement was that it existed not to save man from guilt but to save him from the corruption into which he had fallen after Adam and Eve. Consequently the life was more important than the death. . . . Among the Latin fathers the stress was entirely different. Here the idea was that man was being redeemed, not from corruption primarily, but from guilt. . . . Whereas the Greek theologians regarded God as primarily Absolute Spirit, the Latin theologians regarded God as Governor and Lawgiver, with the mind of a Roman lawyer (their theology tends to be in legalistic terms). (Huxley 1980: 204)

The force of the image changes dramatically as soon as music is perceived in terms of its subjective emotional power rather than simply as acoustic tokens of an orderly existence. As soon as the lion is understood as a symbol of divine leadership (as in heraldic imagery or in the children's fiction of C. S. Lewis) the focus of interpretation shifts from simple acoustic imagery to a musical content of human morality that music communicates. Instead of music representing order and measure, we have music as a means of persuading listeners of a particular life-style and view of humanity, which in turn includes an attitude to the reality of human suffering. Suffering humanity has a different attitude to leadership, and requires an alternative rationale for the death of a leader and the necessary survival in society of the values embodied in leadership.

    Out of this changed interpretation of a musical image of death and resurrection arises the doctrine of the divinity and martyrdom of kings. 'It is usually said [remarked Dean Inge] that the resurrection of the body is a Jewish doctrine, the immortality of the soul a Greek doctrine. But the Jews were very slow to bring the idea of a future life into their living faith. . . . The maturest Greek philosophers regard eternity as the divine mode of existence, while mortals are born, live and die in time. . . . The attempt to hold these very discrepant beliefs together has reduced Christian eschatology to extreme confusion' (Inge, in Livingtone 1928: 54–5).

Historians have been loath to admit that the language used of Augustus might actually be in some ways parallel to that used of Christ. Yet the suggestion is neither absurd nor even blasphemous, for the attempt of Christians to define a historical man as a god was made in a political and religious context transformed by Augustus . . . We can observe something of the process by which the idea of the Saviour was developed at Rome. The pastoral poems of Virgil include one, dated to 40 BC, in the form of a prophecy of the return of the Golden Age (the 'Messianic' Eclogue, 4). The prophecy is attributed to the Sibyl of Cumae, under the inspiration of Apollo. (Wallace-Hadrill 1993: 89–91)

The new doctrine attaches to that aspect of music that so troubled the Greek rationalists, namely its double-edged powers of expression and communication. Through melody, and more importantly the distortions of pitch introduced by a skilled melodist for expressive effect, music is able not only to inspire loyalty and social discipline, but just as easily to trigger the release of emotions of a contagious and socially disruptive kind. Any system of belief that embraces individual responsibility for individual action is bound to reconcile itself with the continuing possibility of dissent, disturbance, error, and change. Virgil's world image in the *Georgics* corresponds to the music of an Aeolian harp, shimmering in the breeze, untouched by human hand, a musical instrument employed as a sensing sevice to intercept and reveal patterns of change in nature. The challenging counter-tradition draws on the musical tradition of King David and his harp, a tradition of suffering, of heroic self-assertion, above all of creative intervention in the existing order. All composed music involves creating a disturbance that has to be justified in terms of the quality of the actions and motives of the performer.

A doctrine of suffering humanity is one that endorses the role of music as a medium of expression ('outing') of intense human emotions. Its consequences, long since predicted by Plato, entail social division, political uncertainty, and belief in individual redemption from a condition of slavery. The curiously English representation of Christ as a lion conscripts the symbolism of a classical devotion to the divine right of an intelligent ruling class into the service of a moral militancy fired by powerful collective emotion. This lion is no mortal beast whose dried sinews angels may pluck, but a living embodiment of autocratic power designed to instil the fear of God in the unbeliever. The Christian myth of death and resurrection is focused on processes and motivations, in contrast to the classical interest in natural materials and how they behave. It would not have occurred to Virgil to apportion blame for the death of a lion, or attribute the virtuous behaviour of bees to a religious conversion. They are merely instruments responding to the play of a poetic intelligence. The crucifixion, on the other hand, focuses attention on the impact on the world order of a morally discordant event provoked by interest groups in society playing on the instrument of government.

16

Discourse

THERE are those who declare music to be unintelligible. Presumably they find it so. Some make unintelligibility a virtue. In the opening sentences of *Music and the Emotions: The Philosophical Theories* Malcolm Budd challenges Rameau's definition of music as the science of sounds, declaring that 'when music is regarded as one of the fine arts it is more accurate to define it . . . as the art of sounds', furthermore, 'the art of uninterpreted sounds' (Budd 1985: ix). In effect, 'I do not think that music, considered as an art, ever does convey propositions of a philosophical kind' (private communication, 1993). I am sure he is not the only philosopher to think so. I also believe that if music could be shown to convey propositions of a philosophical kind, then that would be sufficient proof, in present company, that music is intelligible.

Right away we can eliminate the parenthesis 'considered as an art', for if it means what I think it means, what it means is that considering music as an art (aka listening to Mozart for the sheer pleasure of it) is incompatible with music being listened to as intelligible, which may be true in a majority of cases but is hardly relevant, let alone complimentary. Or alternatively we may take it to mean that music, considered as an art, is valued for beauty, and not for ideas, and therefore to consider music as a vehicle for ideas is a proposition without meaning. The idea that anything considered as art is *ipso facto* not meant to convey ideas would be alarming, were it not so quaint. A third layer of meaning arises from the consideration that music considered as an art produces an emotional response, and emotions are by definition experiences of inarticulate confusion or Schopenhauerian intellectual submission to a higher or more powerful will. But these are matters of the psychology of taste. The question whether music can ever convey propositions of a philosophical kind does not to my mind entail that if it does convey propositions of a philosophical kind it cannot be music.

What then is a proposition of a philosophical kind? In response to the question 'Can Machines Think?' Alan Turing devised 'The Imitation Game' according to which an independent observer decides from two sets of printed factual statements which are the work of a human subject and which are the work of a computer ('Computing Machinery and Intelligence', reproduced in Anderson 1964: 4–24). To a lay reader this is a very specialized definition of thinking, one that leaves out facial cues, tone of voice, emotional colouring, eye contact, etc. Thinking defined as statements on the printed page that make acceptable sense to a supposedly neutral reader is thinking determined by peer adjudication (an uncomfortable reminder that Turing's essay was written in the era of Joe McCarthy, and that peer adjudication of a sort drove Turing himself to an early grave). Peer adjudication is all right as far as it goes, but the definition has nothing to do with what the thought is about, only with the parameters of acceptable self-expression. To my mind, however, the proposition 'Can Machines Think?' means 'are machines capable of reasoning for themselves?', i.e. are they capable of independent decision-making. The correct evaluation of independent decision-making cannot be whether an observer agrees with the machine, but whether the decision manages to be innovative and enterprising as well as internally consistent. Internal consistency is a feature of programming.

A similar danger lies in the formulation that music may or may not convey propositions of a philosophical kind. It attributes a special value to philosophical propositions and expects music to conform to what philosophy understands by a proposition. While I think we can meet this requirement, I do not agree with the implication that music should necessarily conform in order for it to be conceded to convey meaning. We can show that there are statements in music and that they can be subject to a form of logical manipulation. The great achievement of late eighteenth-century music was the development of first-movement form which, in addition to signalling a new awareness of temporal continuity, pioneered a new form of abstract logic. First-movement or sonata form is a determining feature of 'absolute' classical music: sonatas, string quartets, concertos, and symphonies. It consists essentially of an exposition, a development, and a recapitulation. The exposition is concerned with statements of a principal and optional secondary (opposing or complementary) theme. The exposition begins in the tonic key but evolves away from it toward a related key, usually the dominant. The arrival at a new key, representing a change from the initial terms of reference, is summarized by an optional codetta. There follows a development section, in which the themes are anatomized, transposed, and combined in various ways. The recapitulation is a restatement of the themes of the exposition, this time incorporating modifications arrived at during the development, and beginning and ending in the tonic key, with an optional coda summarizing the final point of arrival. In effect, first-movement form subjects one or more initial propositions to critical examination and draws out a variety of options for further development, options that may themselves be organized in a sequence of ascending complexity or abstraction, and ending with a restatement of the initial propositions in a manner conveying a higher sense of their potential for meaning.

In *Style and Idea* (London, 1975), Schoenberg makes the important distinction between a melody and a theme. This is a distinction of which Schopenhauer for one is seemingly unaware ('A melody is a temporal sequence of different tones connected together in a particular way: it is a process with a beginning and an end; its stages are heard in relation to preceding segments of the process and to expected continuations of it; it runs its course and in doing so is grasped as a single entity' (Budd 1985: 87)). A melody is a tune with a beginning, middle, and end. It is complete in itself. A theme, on the other hand, is a musical statement that suggests possibilities of continuation or completion. The art of composing thematically lies in satisfying the listener's appetite for continuation while frustrating the desire for completion.

The opening violin sequence of the Mozart G minor Symphony No. 40 (K. 550) first movement is a case in point. This is the theme that can be approximately rendered in words as a four-line question-and-answer exchange:

1. *Do you want, do you want, do you* | *want to?*
   | Gm (I)

2. —Yes I do, yes I do, yes I | want to;
   | Cm6 (IVc+6 = ii°d+7)

3. *Do you want, do you want, do you* | *want to?*
   | D7 (Vb+7)

4. —Yes I do, yes I do, yes I | want to . . .
   | Gm (I)

Which banality only serves to underline that music is considerably purer in expression and richer in implication than words. To give a full account of the implications of Mozart's opening quatrain, in which the same phrase-rhythm is stated in varying relationships to the underlying G minor key, would take more space than is presently available. For the time being, I need only remark that the phrase itself is structured in the form of a three-times false start ending in a rising sixth, a questioning inflexion. We recognize it as a false start because the entry of the full string orchestra, establishing the tonic key, is delayed until after the third repetition of the anacrusis ('do you | want to?'). Subsequent answering phrases build on the rhythm of the false start, but in ways that convey momentum. The second phrase transforms the repeated anacrusis into a descending 'answering' sequence, accompanied by a chord change from tonic G minor to a tonal suspension on the subdominant C minor, a classic I–IVc progression. The third phrase is a variation of the first, the minor interval of the anacrusis (E flat–D) changed to a more stable major second (D–C), and accompanied by a clever chord progression playing on the ambiguous identity of the comparatively weak added-sixth subdominant C minor, third inversion IVc+6 and its stronger alter ego as supertonic diminished seventh, fourth inversion ii°d+7. The added sixth, A, is a focus of attention both as the contributing dissonance, and as link note to the chord's harmonic consequent, the first inversion dominant chord Vb, D major over F sharp. Moving from the stability of bassline G to an unstable bassline F sharp creates harmonic momentum for a transition to a new stable state, and in the fourth phrase the second-phrase transformation to a descending sequence is repeated, resolving to the original G minor starting-point. There is all the same a discordant feature of the return to home base, the smooth line of descent having been interrupted this time round by an awkward leap from F sharp to E flat, suggesting a forced rather than a natural conclusion. At the end of the quatrain the theme is back where it started, in G minor, resting on the third degree, B flat. This is the same note to which the opening line ascended, but an octave lower. In effect, the verse ends with the original question still poised on B flat, waiting for an answer. This is only part of the meaning of the passage. The contributions of tempo, phrasing, and instrumentation remain still to be addressed.

Webern's Op. 27 *Variations* for piano first movement is an example of classical first-movement exposition operating outside the framework of classical tonality. The brief exposition is based on degrees of symmetry between alternate right- and left-hand phrases. Each phrase is a triangular formation consisting of a two-note interval followed by a single note, or the reverse. A phrase can either expand from one note to a two-note interval, or contract from a two-note interval to one note. The time-span of a phrase is either four beats long: 'start – two – three – stop', or two beats long: 'start – stop'. When two phrases coincide and one is long and the other short, the short triangle can be enclosed by, and interact with, the long triangle, producing additional internal 'rhymes'.

The range of potential symmetries is considerable: right hand/ left hand, high/low, forward/back, same/different, right way up/inverted, included/ excluded; in addition the position of the single note in relation to its complementary two-note interval can express a further variety of relationships including inside/outside, above/below, antecedent/consequent, and eventually louder/softer. What is being discussed here in purely musical terms is the richness of possible symmetries and variations that can be expressed in the simplest of note formations. Webern's affinity for triangles suggests the purity of Pythagorean geometry and the abstract formality of mathematical logic. The music retains, however, a sense of Mozartean momentum directly comparable with the example from the G minor Symphony, a rhythm based on a visual syncopation between the cadence of individual phrases (which seem to be in duple time) in opposition to a written time signature of three beats to the bar. As Mozart sets a question-and-answer rhythm of phrasing against a slower, syncopated rhythm of chord changes, so Webern sets his serially based phrases in oscillatory motion against the unstated lilt of a Viennese waltz.

That is all very well, the voice in the audience murmurs, but what is the meaning in these musical phrases? How do they relate to the serious concerns of philosophy? It is understandable that those who have a stake in what Marcelo Dascal calls 'the assumption of a structural convergence between language and thought' (Dascal 1983: 7) should view with alarm the possibility that music is in there with a chance as well. Certainly music is capable of functioning symbolically, as Hesse envisaged in *The Glass Bead Game*. Any scale of values, or any alphanumeric code, can be manipulated in terms of notes of music: Berg incorporates coded messages in *The Lyric Suite* and Messiaen transliterates sacred texts in *Le Mystère de la Sainte Trinité*. But codes are not thoughts. We have to find the thoughts that inhere and connect in musical sounds.

Thoughts are what you think, but not all of what you think is expressed as thoughts. The expression of thoughts requires two things: organized distinctions, and a medium of articulation. For most intellectuals the medium is language, but there are other forms of expression including facial and body gesture, dress, sport, photography, painting, and music. If language is not the only medium of expression then thinking may have to be redefined in terms of objectives rather than forms. The propositions of philosophy are concerned *au fond* with such issues as consciousness, the self in relation to the world, principles of action, communication, the nature of time, values, government, altruism, and so on. Rather than attempting to reconcile music with the inflections of speech and the conventions of language, we may ask whether music is able to convey such basic ideas as self, the world, and time in alternative terms, and if so, whether the terms are intelligible to ordinary mortals or operate on a primitive, subliminal level. There are two ways of answering. First, that music addresses these fundamental issues essentially through what it is, and only consequently through what it purports to say. The knowledge that comes with listening to music entails a prior acceptance of the very issues that words on the printed page labour often in vain to affirm. Music is a temporal process. Hearing a note of a particular pitch is acknowledging an acoustic process and associated detection and evaluation mechanisms that do not simply postulate, but absolutely require a conception of reality that is cyclical, temporal, and predictable. These things are manifest. To practical musicians ontology, or 'the business of is-ness', is not an issue, or rather, is only a visual, language-related problem, which may help to explain why musicians are usually better at making music than talking about it.

One of the interesting consequences of post-1945 abstraction in art and music has been a revival of popular awareness of the philosophical dimension of artistic activity. The artwork, in the portfolio of an Andy Warhol or a John Cage, is reconstituted as a cultural statement or proposition to be understood in the context of an over-specialized Western European philosophical tradition that has reduced the status of art to the merely decorative, anecdotal, and invincibly personal. This intellectual strain of American art has flourished by virtue of the challenge it offers to conventional definitions of what art is about, though it risks being tedious to those for whom conventional definitions no longer apply. The tension between overt and implicit meanings continues to be explored, for example, in the sublime kitsch of Jeff Koons and the Philip Glass symphony after David Bowie (though in the latter instance Bowie appears to have had the last word).

Among European composers of the post-war generation, the serialization of musical parameters came as a response to new insights provided by the tape medium into the nature and composition of musical sounds and noises, entailing a new sensibility toward instrumental sounds, their acoustical relationships and perceptual implications. Against the prevailing attitude to composition as essentially an activity of notational calculation and design, to which instrumentation added an arbitrary gloss, advanced composers came to understand more clearly, and learned to exploit, the processes of sound production responsible for the differences between musical sounds, and their formal implications. While not constituting a language, the resulting play of serially organized distinctions allowed a number of composers a new precision in determining auditory priorities which can be interpreted, in my view, as defining individual philosophies. Examples to hand are *Le Marteau sans maître* by Boulez, *Introitus* by Stravinsky, and *Refrain* by Stockhausen. In all three works the choice of instrumentation has formal significance.

A setting of verses by René Char, *Le Marteau* is composed for contralto voice, alto flute, viola, guitar, xylorimba, vibraphone, and percussion. The instrumentation serves a dual agenda, a simple opposition of pitched versus unpitched sounds, corresponding to the consonants and vowels of a sung (and occasionally spoken) text, and a more subtle and elaborate scheme of relationships connecting the pitched instruments as a group. All share the same contralto range, and they function as 'phase-locations' in a cycle of timbres leading from the voice, which is the most completely articulate instrument (continuous legato, combining 'wind' and 'strings' (vocal cords), and comprehending language, melody, vowel harmonies, and percussive consonants), through stages of impoverishment and transformation via viola (wood and strings, continuous legato, melody and harmony, also percussion (pizzicato), voice-like but without language), guitar (wood and strings, pitch-percussion, no continuous legato, pizzicato melody and harmony), xylorimba (wood percussion, stick action, no continuous legato, little sustain), vibraphone (metal percussion, ringing sounds, enhanced sustain, mechanical vibrato), alto flute (metal wind, natural vibrato, natural sustain, melody but no harmony, voice-like expression) back to the voice again. The subtext of *Le Marteau*, therefore, is the singing and speaking voice as expressing the *fons et origo* of an entire vocabulary of musical distinctions of which the repertoire of ancillary instruments represent residual fragments. The meaning of the subtext is the declared affinity of poetic language via speech and song with the sounds and terms of musical expression, which is to say that the world (or the poet's conception of it) is comprehended not in the meaning of a poetic text alone, but in the act of vocalization itself.

Stravinsky's *Introitus* is instrumentated in a similar fashion, this time taking the male tenor-bass voice range rather than the female contralto as its point of departure. The composer employs a comparable repertoire of timbres, but where Boulez's members are single, Stravinsky's are paired: tenors/basses, viola/contrabass, high/low timpani, high/low tam-tams, harp/piano. Like Boulez, Stravinsky draws on instrumental contrasts that describe a continuum leading from the singing/speaking voice (embodying text, pitch, sustain, phrasing) via bowed strings (pitch, sustain), timpani (muffled pitch, tremolo sustain), tam-tams (indeterminate pitch, reverberation) to harp and piano (harmony, reverberation). Stravinsky's subtext is the transition from vocal line to keyboard harmony, corresponding to a shift of focus from the text and linear time (mortality) to vertical instantaneity: the image of eternity implicit in the harp and piano chords that punctuate the 'Requiescat' and are left in suspense 'when soft voices die'.

Stockhausen's *Refrain* is a composition for a trio of keyboards (piano, celesta, glockenspiel, ancillary percussion) that brings a different perception to bear on the decay of pitched percussion sounds. For Boulez, the focus of musical expression is the onset or attack, in a serial universe consisting of elements fixed in predetermined positions in pitch, timbre, and time; in the Boulez tradition, duration and liaison between successive elements are not intrinsic features of this universe but rather a consequence of human activity making connections, either voluntarily (bowing and phrasing) or with the aid of a text (song). For Stravinsky, decay of sound signifies both a fading of conscious awareness and also human mortality: 'the evanescence of all things'. For Stockhausen, however, sounds dying away are consciously understood as a dynamic process; *Refrain* focuses, as a matter of principle, on the relation of the length of time a sound may last, to the strength of its initial attack, and the reverberation characteristic of the instrument (the piano is inherently more reverberant than the glockenspiel, and the glockenspiel than the celesta). What this tells us is not that different instruments represent different states of being, but that they embody different capacities to endure. Endurance itself becomes a matter of will. The music is timed, not with reference to a beat or a time signature, but by how long it takes for a given note on a given instrument to decay from an initial loudness to a specified dynamic. In the composition, these moments of seemingly frozen time are interrupted by periodic dissolves into amorphous textures of superimposed grace notes taken as fast as possible. Time is thus polarized between the virtual eternity of waiting for something to happen, and the chaos of everything happening at once.

Reflecting on the varied responses of post-encephalitic patients to treatment with L-DOPA, Oliver Sacks acknowledges the wholeness of human personality as a normally dynamic 'ontological continuum' capable of fragmentation under stress into 'sharply-differentiated "equivalents" of being' occupying a mental inner space 'where there is succession without extension, moments without time, and change without transit: in short, the world of quantum mechanics' (Sacks 1973: 220 n). Whatever other meanings they convey, the three compositions of Boulez, Stravinsky, and Stockhausen clearly postulate an auditory 'ontological continuum' within which the musical focus fluctuates between a sense and an imagery of wholeness and harmony, and affective splits or decompositions of being. The music is 'about' how that proposition is understood. 'Quantum mechanics requires, [said] Heisenberg, a modality which is situated between logical possibility and actuality, which he calls "potentia" . . . [In] considering the question of what happens between two observations, Heisenberg's answer is "the term 'happens' is restricted to the observation" ' (Shimony 1993: 313). How the listener responds to this music, whether it is perceived as coherent or chaotic, is a measure of individual strategies and propensities. That, too, is an answer.

Envoi

IN *The Sense of Order* Ernst Gombrich recalls Plato's account in *Phaedo* of the condemned Socrates urging his disciples not to grieve at his death because the soul is immortal.

> He introduces this particular argument by asking one of his pupils whether he knows what 'likeness' is. And yet, how can he know? Had he ever seen two things which were absolutely alike—for instance two pieces of chalk or of wood which could be so described? If not, his knowledge of the idea or concept of likeness could not derive from sense experience. It must come from elsewhere. We must have seen or experienced mathematical equality before our soul ever entered into our bodies, and it is this memory that provides us with the standard by which we judge whether things in this world are more or less alike.
>
> I once had a student who cried when she read this poignant scene because she could not bear the thought of Socrates grounding his hopes of immortality on a fallacy. (Gombrich 1984: 113)

Four versions of Socrates compete for attention in this one anecdote. There is Socrates' argument for the immortality of the soul, which has not survived; there is Plato's surviving account of Socrates' argument; there is Gombrich's account of Plato's account; and there is the dismay of Gombrich's student that Socrates should have believed such a story.

Plato's version has the hallmarks of an account at second hand. The basic elements appear authentic enough: we can take it as true that Socrates under sentence of death tried to console his disciples by saying that the soul was immortal, and that he used an argument from human knowledge of 'absolute likeness' as distinct from human experience that can only admit relative similarities. The trouble with this argument is not so much that it is a fallacy as that as reported it doesn't fit the case to be made. Perhaps Socrates did draw an analogy from mathematics, but I think Plato has substituted his own preferred mathematical analogy for the one Socrates would have been more likely to employ. Plato makes Socrates appear to say that a sense of absolute likeness is god-given, and that is proof of a higher plane of existence to which those with the knowledge of absolute likeness can therefore claim entry. As a visual arts historian, Gombrich sees no reason to comment on Socrates' examples of the inadequacy of evidence for absolute likeness in normal sensory experience, that we never actually see pieces of wood or chalk that are identical.

But visual experience is not the whole story. There is something missing. Mathematics is the clue, because mathematics implies musical acoustics, the relationship of measure and pitch. Once music enters the equation Socrates' message takes on an entirely new meaning. We can picture the scene, with Socrates in conversation with his disciples. There is a musician present. What takes place is philosophical debate interspersed with expressions of regret and consolation. From time to time Socrates illustrates his lesson with diagrams sketched in chalk on a slate. At one point they sing together. It could be a hymn to the gods, or a drinking song for old times. In the pause after the song has ended Socrates takes the lyre from the musician and runs his hand over the strings. He asks, what have we just been doing? What does this music mean, that we know so well, and can sing together? Surely what it means is the existence of a higher reality, an immortal reality, that we all acknowledge and can all aspire to. That knowledge is in the pitches and intervals contained in the strings of the lyre. No two voices are alike, and yet they can achieve a perfect unison. Where is the equivalent unanimity in material experience? No two marks of chalk (pointing to the slate) or instruments of wood (indicating the lyre) could ever express such a degree of likeness. The world is governed by visual concepts of likeness, which lead to the imposition of conformity and the suppression of true freedom of thought. But the voice is the messenger of the soul, not the body, and if the voice can express absolute likeness, then the soul is truly independent of the body, and is certain to survive after death.

References

AARONS, MAUREEN, and GITTENS, TESSA (1992) *The Handbook of Autism: A Guide for Parents and Professionals*, London.

ANDERSON, ALLAN ROSS (ed.) (1964), *Minds and Machines*, Englewood Cliffs, NJ.

ARISTOTLE (1955), *Ethics*, trans. J. A. K. Thomson, Harmondsworth.

—— (1994), *Posterior Analytics*, trans. with a commentary by Jonathan Barnes, 2nd edn., Oxford.

ARPS, BERNARD (ed.) (1993), *Performance in Java and Bali: Studies of Narrative, Theatre, Music, and Dance*, London.

AUGUSTINE (1907), *Confessions*, trans. E. B. Pusey, London.

AYER, A. J. (1984), *Philosophy in the Twentieth Century*, London.

BALLANTYNE, DEBORAH (1990), *Handbook of Audiological Techniques*, London.

BARBER, CHARLES (1993), *The English Language: A Historical Introduction* (Cambridge Approaches to Linguistics), Cambridge.

BARKER, ANDREW (1991), 'Plato and Aristoxenus on *Melos*', in Burnett *et al.* 1991.

BERANEK, LEO L. (1966), 'Noise', *Scientific American*, 215/6.

BLOOM, LOIS (1993), *The Transition from Infancy to Language: Acquiring the Power of Expression*, Cambridge.

BOLINGER, DWIGHT (ed.) (1972), *Intonation: Selected Readings* (Penguin Modern Linguistics Readings), Harmondsworth.

BOOTZIN, RICHARD R., and ACOCELLA, JOAN ROSS (1988), *Abnormal Psychology: Current perspectives*, 5th edn., New York.

BRÜMMER, VINCENT (1993), *The Model of Love: A Study in Philosophical Theology*, Cambridge.

BUDD, MALCOLM (1985), *Music and the Emotions: The Philosophical Theories* (International Library of Philosophy), London.

BURN, A. R. (1966), *The Pelican History of Greece*, Harmondsworth.

BURNETT, CHARLES (1991), 'Sound and its Perception in the Middle Ages', in Burnett *et al.* 1991.

—— FEND, MICHAEL, and GOUK, PENELOPE (eds.) (1991), *The Second*

Sense: Studies in Hearing and Musical Judgement from Antiquity to the Seventeenth Century (Warburg Institute Surveys and Texts 22), London.

CARRUTHERS, PETER (1986), *Introducing Persons: Theories and Arguments in the Philosophy of Mind*, London.

CERULO, KAREN A. (1992), 'Putting it together: measuring the syntax of aural and visual symbols', in Robert Wuthnow (ed.), *Vocabularies of Public Life: Empirical Essays in Symbolic Structure*, London.

CHOMSKY, NOAM (1984), *Modular Approaches to the Study of the Mind*, San Diego.

CLANCHY, M. T. (1993), *From Memory to Written Record: England 1066–1307*, 2nd edn., Oxford.

CRITCHLEY, MACDONALD, and HENSON, R. A. (eds.) (1977), *Music and the Brain*, London.

CROMBIE, A. C. (1994), *Styles of Scientific Thinking in the European Tradition: The History of Argument and Explanation Especially in the Mathematical and Biomedical Sciences and Arts*, London.

DAMASIO, A. R., and DAMASIO, H. (1977), 'The Musical faculty and cerebral dominance', in Critchley and Henson 1977.

DASCAL, MARCELO (1983), *Pragmatics and the Philosophy of Mind I: Thought in Language* (Pragmatics & Beyond), Amsterdam.

DAVIES, PAUL C. W., and BROWN, JULIAN (eds.) (1988), *Superstrings: A Theory of Everything?*, Cambridge.

DEBUSSY, CLAUDE (1962), 'Monsieur Croche the Dilettante Hater', trans. B. N. Langdon Davies, in Debussy *et al.* 1962.

—— BUSONI, FERRUCCIO, and IVES, CHARLES E. (1962), *Three Classics in the Aesthetics of Music*, New York.

DEUTSCH, DIANA (1977), 'Memory and attention in music', in Critchley and Henson 1977.

DICKINSON, G. LOWES (1920), *The Greek View of Life*, 13th edn., New York.

DUMMETT, MICHAEL (1993), *Origins of Analytical Philosophy*, London.

ELIOT, T. S. (1963), *Selected Prose*, ed. John Hayward, new edn., Harmondsworth.

FIELD, J.V. (1993), 'Piero della Francesca and Perspective', in Field and James 1993.

—— and JAMES, FRANK A. J. L. (eds.) (1993), *Renaissance and Revolution: Humanists, Scholars, Craftsmen and Natural Philosophers in Early Modern Europe*, Cambridge.

FISCH, L. (1987), *Investigating Hearing in Children*, London.

FITZPATRICK, P. J. (1993), *In Breaking of Bread: The Eucharist and Ritual*, Cambridge.

FOGELIN, ROBERT J. (1976), *Wittgenstein*, London.

GARDNER, MARTIN (1978), 'White and brown music, fractal curves and one-over-f fluctuations', *Scientific American*, 238/4.

GELL, ALFRED (1992), *The Anthropology of Time: Cultural Constructions of Temporal Maps and Images*, Oxford.

GIANNINI, TULA (1993), *Great Flute Makers of France: The Lot and Godfroy families 1650–1900*, London.

GILLBERG, CHRISTOPHER, and COLEMAN, MARY (1992), *The Biology of the Autistic Syndromes*, 2nd edn. (Clinics in Developmental Medicine No. 126), London.

GLEASON, JEAN BERKO (1993), 'Neurolinguistic aspects of a first language', in Hyltenstam and Viberg 1993.

GOMBRICH, ERNST H. (1984), *The Sense of Order: A Study in the Psychology of Decorative Art* (The Wrightsman Lectures), 2nd edn., New York.

GUNDERSON, KEITH (1985), *Mentality and Machines: A Survey of the Artificial Intelligence Debate*, 2nd edn., Minneapolis.

HABGOOD, JOHN (1993), *Making Sense*, London.

HANFLING, OSWALD (1989), *Wittgenstein's Later Philosophy*, Basingstoke.

HARRINGTON, BENJAMIN (1961), *Greek Science: Its Meaning for Us*, rev. edn., Harmondsworth.

HARRIS-WARRICK, REBECCA (1993), 'Interpreting pendulum markings for French Baroque dances', *Historical Performance* 6/1: 9–22.

HILL, DONALD R. (1993), *Islamic Science and Engineering*, Edinburgh.

HOOD, J. D. (1977), 'Psychological and physiological aspects of hearing', in Critchley and Henson 1977.

HOWE, LEO, and WAIN, ALAN (1993), *Predicting the Future* (Darwin College Lectures), Cambridge.

HUFFMAN, CARL A. (1993), *Philolaus of Croton, Pythagorean and Presocratic: A Commentary on the Fragments and Testimonia with Interpretive Essays*, Cambridge.

HUXLEY, ALDOUS (1980), *The Human Situation: Lectures at Santa Barbara, 1959*, ed. Piero Ferruci, London.

HYLTENSTAM, KENNETH, and VIBERG, ÅKE (eds.) (1993), *Progression and Regression in Language: Sociocultural, Neuropsychological, & Linguistic Perspectives*, Cambridge.

JEANS, JAMES (1937), *Science and Music*, Cambridge.

—— (1950), *The Growth of Physical Science*, Cambridge.

JOHNSTON, IAN (1989), *Measured Tones: The Interplay of Physics and Music*, Bristol.

JONES, MARK (ed.) (1992), *Why Fakes Matter: Essays on Problems of Authenticity*, London.

JUBIEN, MICHAEL (1993), *Ontology, Modality, and the Fallacy of Reference*, Cambridge.

KARAJAN, HERBERT VON (1989), *My Autobiography as Told to Franz Endler*, trans. Stewart Spencer, London.

KITTO, H. D. F. (1951), *The Greeks*, Harmondsworth.

KÖHLER, WOLFGANG (1959), *Gestalt Psychology: An Introduction to New Concepts in Modern Psychology*, New York.

KUHN, THOMAS S. (1993), 'Metaphor in science', in Ortony 1993.

LAPEDES, DANIEL N. (ed.) (1978), *McGraw-Hill Dictionary of Scientific and Technical Terms*, 2nd edn., New York.

LAVER, JOHN (1994), *Principles of Phonetics*, Cambridge.

LEIBER, JUSTIN (1993), *Paradoxes* (Interpretations series), London.

LÉON, PIERRE R., and MARTIN, PHILIPPE (1972), 'Machines and measurements', in Bolinger 1972.

LEVINSON, STEPHEN E., and LIBERMAN, MARK Y. (1981), 'Speech recognition by computer', *Scientific American* 244/4.

LING, DANIEL (1976), *Speech and the Hearing-Impaired Child: Theory and Practice*, Washington.

LIVINGSTONE, R. W. (ed.) (1921), *The Legacy of Greece*, Oxford.

—— (1928), *The Mission of Greece: Some Greek Views of Life in the Roman World*, Oxford.

McCALL, STORRS (1994), *A Model of the Universe: Space-time, Probability, and Decision*, Oxford.

McNEILL, DAVID (1978), 'Speech and thought', in Ivana Markova (ed.), *The Social Context of Language*, New York.

MACONIE, ROBIN (1990), *The Concept of Music*, Oxford.

—— and CUNNINGHAM, CHRIS (1978), 'Computers unveil the shape of melody', *New Scientist*, 94/1302, London.

McSHANE, JOHN (1980), *Learning to Talk*, Cambridge.

MEYER, JÜRGEN (1978), *Acoustics and the Performance of Music*, trans J. Bowsher and S. Westphal, Frankfurt am Main.

NOHAIN, JEAN, and CARADEC, F. (1992), *Petomane 1857–1945*, new edn., London.

OLSON, DAVID R. (1994), *The World on Paper: The Conceptual and Cognitive Implications of Writing and Reading*, Cambridge.

ORTONY, ANDREW (ed.) (1993), *Metaphor and Thought*, 2nd edn., Cambridge.

PALISCA, CLAUDE V. (1985), *Humanism in Italian Renaissance Musical Thought*, New Haven.

PARSONS, DENYS (1975), *Directory of Tunes and Musical Themes*, London.

—— (1992), 'A Remarkable type of conformity in composers' incipits', *The Music Review*, 51/2.

PLATO (1993), *Phaedo*, ed. C. J. Rowe, Cambridge.

—— (1941), *The Republic*, trans. Francis Macdonald Cornford, Oxford.

POTTER, RALPH K., KOPP, GEORGE A., and KOPP, HARRIET GREEN (1966), *Visible Speech*, new edn., New York.

READ, HERBERT (1953), *Art and Industry*, London.

ROEDERER, JUAN G. (1994), *The Physics and Psychophysics of Music: An Introduction*, 3rd edn., New York.

ROTH, LEON (1929), *Spinoza*, London, (repr. 1954).

SACKS, OLIVER (1973), *Awakenings*, London.

SCHNEIDER, ALBRECHT, and BEURMANN, ANDREAS E. (1993), 'Notes on the acoustics and tuning of *gamelan* instruments', in Arps 1993.

SCHOENBERG, ARNOLD (1964), *Letters*, ed. Leonard Stein, London.

—— (1975), *Style and Idea*, ed. Leonard Stein, London.

SEARLE, JOHN (1984), *Minds, Brains and Science: The 1984 Reith Lectures*, London.

SEARS, ELIZABETH (1991), 'The Iconography of Auditory Perception in the Early Middle Ages: On Psalm Illustration and Psalm Exegesis', in Burnett *et al.* 1991.

SHIMONY, ABNER (1993), *Search for a Naturalistic World View*, ii: *Natural Science and Metaphysics*, Cambridge.

SIMPLICIUS (1994), *On Aristotle Physics 7*, trans. Charles Hagen, London.

SKIRBEKK, GUNNAR (1993), *Rationality and Modernity: Essays in Philosophical Pragmatics*, Oslo.

SMALL, ARNOLD M. (1978), *Elements of Hearing Science*, New York.

SORRELL, TOM (ed.) (1993), *The Rise of Modern Philosophy: The Tension between the New and Traditional Philosophies from Machiavelli to Leibniz*, Oxford.

STEWART, IAN (1993), 'Chaos', in Howe and Wain 1993.

STORR, ANTHONY (1992), *Music and the Mind*, London.

STRAVINSKY, IGOR, and CRAFT, ROBERT (1959), *Memories and Commentaries*, London.

STURROCK, JOHN (1993), *The Language of Autobiography: Studies in the First Person Singular*, Cambridge.

TAYLOR, C. C. W. (1987), 'Hellenistic ethics', in Julia Annas (ed.), *Oxford Studies in Ancient Philosophy V*, Oxford.

TOWEY, ALAN (1991), 'Aristotle and Alexander on Hearing and Instantaneous Change: A Dilemma in Aristotle's Account of Hearing', in Burnett *et al.* 1991.

TURING, ALAN M. (1964), 'Computing machinery and intelligence', *Mind*, 59 No. 236 (1950), reprod. in Anderson 1964.

TURNER, JAMES GRANTHAM (ed.) (1993), *Sexuality and Gender in Early Modern Europe: Institutions, Texts, Images*, Cambridge.

VALBERG, J. J. (1992), *The Puzzle of Experience*, Oxford.

WALKER, D. P. (1978), *Studies in Musical Science in the Late Renaissance*, London.

WALLACE-HADRILL, ANDREW (1993), *Augustan Rome* (Classical World series), Bristol.

WARDHALGH, RONALD (1993), *Investigating Language: Central Problems in Linguistics*, Oxford.

WILLIAMS, C. F. ABDY (1903), *The Story of Notation*, London.

WING, HERBERT DANIEL, and BENTLEY, ARNOLD (1966), 'The Mystery of Music', *New Scientist*, 306–7.

YOUNG, J. Z. (1960), *Doubt and Certainty in Science*, rev. edn., New York.

—— (1987), *Philosophy and the Brain*, Oxford.

Index